Stumbling Tou *ard God*

A Prodigal's Return

by Margaret D. McGee

1ST PRIZE WINNER FOR NONFICTION, PACIFIC
NORTHWEST WRITERS ASSOCIATION LITERARY AWARDS

Publication Date: May 2002
Title: Stumbling Toward God
Subtitle: A Prodigal's Return
Author: Margaret D. McGee
Category: Spirituality
Pages: 160
Trim Size: 6 x 9
ISBN: 1-880913-55-0
Price: $15.95, trade paperback original

Innisfree Press, Inc.
Philadelphia, Pennsylvania

Distributed to the general trade by
CONSORTIUM BOOK SALES & DISTRIBUTION

Distributed to the religious trade by INNISFREE PRESS.

Published by Innisfree Press, Inc.
136 Roumfort Road
Philadelphia, PA 19119
800-367-5872
Visit our website at www.InnisfreePress.com

Cover design by Hugh Duffy, PhD Design, Carneys Point, NJ

Library of Congress Cataloging-in-Publication Data
TO BE ADDED

Dedication
TO BE ADDED

Acknowledgments

This book could not have been written without the experiences I had at St. Paul's and the Quimper Fellowship. However, *Stumbling Toward God* is about my own spiritual journey and no one else's. For that reason and in respect for their privacy, I changed the names and some characteristics of some members of my churches who appear in this book. They know who they are, and they have my thanks.

Table of Contents

I. An Atheist Who Prays
    Ripe for grace
    Between anger and awe

II. Ready for Revolution
    Child of altar and blackboard
    Saved by Jesus and my mom
    Saved by the insect world
    Ready for revolution

III. Dreadful Religion
    I've been burned before . . .
    . . . and I won't be burned again

IV. Church Shopping
    A little redemption
    King Midas and the mind-body problem
    What is attractive?

V. Getting to Know You
    Getting to know the Episcopalians
    Getting to know the Unitarians

VI. Liturgy, History, and Ritual
    Juggling the prayer book
    Grappling with the Creed
    The real presence
    Heretics and cliff-jumpers
    A daisy and a sage blossom

VII. Dear God
    From mighty love to nothing at all
    Casting about for God's image
    An unintentional God
    Dressing the emperor

VIII. Grappling with Myth
    Rewriting scripture
    Becoming human with Adam and Eve
    Liberated by myth

IX. From the Virgin to the Cross
    If Mary was a virgin . . .
    Heaven, hell, and the orange peel
    The cross, the cigarette, and me
    Acting out redemption

X. Return
    Paying attention
    God of justice, God of truth

Epilogue: The Episcopalians and the Unitarians

Other Interesting Books

Stumbling Toward God

Chapter I

An Atheist Who Prays

In the fall of 1986, I was an atheist. All the same, I wrote this prayer:

> *Dear God, sustain me in my hour of need.*
> *Stay with me; be my friend.*
> *When I misstep, light my path.*
> *When I hurt, comfort me.*
> *Help me see that I'm not the only one in pain.*
> *Give me the strength to accept myself for what I am.*
> *Amen.*

I didn't believe the universe was created by the deliberate act of a sentient Being. I believed that no such Being watched over us, heard or responded to our prayers, loved us, felt joy when we were good or sorrow when we were bad, or felt anything at all for that matter.

Holding that opinion, I wrote my prayer. After writing it, I cried and felt better. I read it again the next day, taped it to my computer monitor, and prayed it on an almost-daily basis for weeks. As an atheist, what did I think I was doing?

The only thing I knew was that something had changed inside me. Like many people who have a paradoxical experience with God, I was in a mess—a mess that involved other people—and looking for a way out.

A year previously, I had been invited to join the board of a regional writer's conference. I got the invitation in response to an angry letter I wrote to the board president explaining what was wrong with the way they did things. I didn't have much experience with board work at that time, so it was a big surprise to me when they responded to my angry letter by asking me to join up and solve all their problems. I accepted the invitation. I was eager to do good.

As it turned out, I hated virtually every aspect of board work: the endless phone calls and meetings, the political gymnastics required to get more than one person to agree to anything, the shocking realization that not everyone on the board saw me as their savior. After the first year of my three-year term, half of me longed to resign. The other half was sick at the thought. It wouldn't be the first time I quit a worthy project because I couldn't take the heat. Was I incapable of teamwork? Too sensitive to get things done with other people? I admired people who succeeded in work like this. Was I too small to be one of them?

One afternoon, having fielded the third phone call that told me second-hand what some other committee member thought of my latest idea, I sat at my desk, put my head in my hands, and said, *"Dear God. Dear God, help me."* Then I lifted my head, picked up a pen, and wrote the prayer.

Right away, I felt different. As if I'd been drowning in stormy waters and my flailing arms struck something buoyant. Or as if a cool sheet had fallen over me during a fevered dream. The next day when I read the prayer again, I felt better again. I tinkered with the wording a bit, but the essential message didn't change. I felt as if this prayer had been given to me. It was easy to write, unlike other things I write. I felt that the prayer engaged me in a two-way conversation. My side of the conversation had content. The other side didn't have any content that I could tell, but neither was it like talking to a blank wall. The conversation moved me from one place to another. It changed me.

Ripe for grace

I was in trouble when I wrote that prayer, and the prayer helped. It contained the elements I needed to calm down and focus. It reminded me that I wouldn't find my way out of the forest until I admitted I was lost. It helped me remember that other people hurt as much as I do, which helped me forgive them for the pain I thought they caused me. And finally, it gave me permission to be myself. To accept myself. Which was not to say, "I guess I'm just a screw up. I can accept that!" No, I had to face wrongs and try to get them right. But when I did that and at the same time accepted myself in all my fallibility, a glimmer of light appeared in the distance, and I wasn't lost anymore.

In retrospect, the prayer seems wiser than I was at the time—wiser than I am today. I have a certain amount of common sense, but I'm not a dependable source of eternal truths. At the moment I wrote that prayer, I was about as far from eternal truth as you can get.

It had been years since I'd thought or read much about religion, so the underlying principles in the prayer weren't on my mind. I resented the people I worked with and their interference in my plans. I hated my job on the writer's board and longed to quit. The only thing that stopped me was an intense desire not to fail, or not to appear to fail.

This was not the mountain top where sages see clearly; this was the tangled bog where fools trip and fall in the muck.

And yet the situation was ripe for grace. It's easy to see the signs of a fruit ready to fall: the brittle stem, the yellowed skin. I thought I knew best, a frame of mind begging for a fall. I was brittle with anger, and anger is not a bad starting point on the road to grace. Also, I was pushing for change. Mostly I wanted to change other people, but I knew it might be good for me to change, too.

I just didn't expect to suffer in the transformation.

Writing that prayer changed me. I didn't suddenly become the ideal team player. I was still perfectly able to screw up, trip over toes, make dumb decisions. However, when I said that prayer and meant it, I could forgive my enemy. Having forgiven my enemy, I could work with him without driving myself nuts. In the practice of prayer, I had found a tool that helped me grow.

Armed with my prayer, I served out my term on the board, accomplished some of my goals, and then got out of there. Throughout that time, my personal opinion about omnipotent, omniscient Beings stayed the same. In my opinion, no such Being had ever existed or ever would. Regardless, the prayer helped me.

I had become an atheist who prays.

Between anger and awe

Engaged in a two-way conversation that started out "Dear God" and ended up "Amen," how could I call myself an atheist?

To me, the word "God" meant Somebody who deliberately created the universe, loves it, and pays attention. Like a good father. As long as that was my definition, I was an atheist, because it seemed clear to me that no such Being existed. If I was wrong and It did exist, then I thought It had a lot to answer for.

In my childhood, I was lucky: I had a good father. He loved me and my brother and sister, and we knew it. He worked hard to provide for his family. We had adequate food and clothing. We felt safe in our home. My father had high expectations for his children and let us know what they were. When we didn't meet them, he let us know that, too. He set a good example: he worked hard and told the truth. My father isn't perfect. He's only human, not a god. But he was, and is, a good father, so I felt I had a basis for comparison.

When I observed the world, it didn't seem to me that I was observing the household of a good father. In fact, God's "fathering" appeared to me like the random acts of an alcoholic nightmare. One child favored, the next condemned. All the explanations for suffering and evil in the world, all the alibis that people have written for God over the millennia. "You call this *love*?" I'd ask the nonexistent Being. "You call this *paying attention*? Did you make this place, or not? Are you responsible for your actions, or what?"

I remained an atheist while I prayed. Even though I started my prayer with "Dear God," I definitely was not praying to that incompetent, all-powerful Being. I didn't know what I was praying to, I just knew it wasn't *That*.

Weeks and months passed while I continued to pray as an atheist. I noticed myself changing in other ways. I cried more often at the movies. I was more often struck with wonder and awe: at a sunset, a piece of fabric, a song lyric.

> *You must remember this,*
> *A kiss is still a kiss,*
> *A sigh is just a sigh.*
> *The fundamental things apply*
> *As time goes by.*

I listened to those lyrics and wondered how anything so simple and obvious could cut so deep.

During part of this time I worked as a writer at software companies, including the Microsoft Corporation. My job involved going to meetings where we defined new software products. At those meetings, I watched with increasing interest how difficult human communication is, how often it fails. Even when the people trying to communicate were smart, articulate, and motivated, almost every first attempt to explain a new idea failed. Listeners didn't understand the new idea when they first heard it, and they argued against the idea based on their misunderstandings of it.

Yet we kept at it, we didn't give up, we kept slogging away. We tried again and again to explain our ideas, to understand the other ideas at the table and put them together into something greater than any of us could achieve alone. I saw I was part of a process larger than myself. I was astonished and humbled at the effort humans were willing to put into this process. It is endearing, this dogged determination of the human species to communicate with each other, even though we aren't very good at it.

Eventually, I left the software business to write about other things. My husband, David, and I moved to a house in the country surrounded by woods and cow pastures. Here, too, everyday tasks and experiences became catalysts for this increasing sense of awe. As part of our transition into country life, I built a compost bin in our back yard. I fed the compost bin on dirt and weeds from the yard, fruit and vegetable scraps from our kitchen, and an occasional shovelful of manure from a neighbor's barn. Every few months, I turned my compost pile—that is, I used a pitchfork to put the top stuff on the bottom and the bottom stuff on the top. It was hard work, plying the pitchfork. Whenever I stopped to rest, the rich, sweet odor of new earth enveloped me. I leaned against the pitchfork, looked down, and watched the moving microcosm of beetles, millipedes, worms, and other small creatures that had changed my garbage into new earth. Someday their descendants would probably change me into new earth, too.

Again, I felt part of a process larger than myself, but now the process was more than human. It spanned time from start to finish, and it spanned all space and matter, too. Again, I was struck with awe, and in this case also filled with a curious sense of peace.

I'd moved into a "thin place" in the span of my life, a place where the curtain between the visible and the invisible worlds grows thin, and one becomes aware, if only subliminally, of movement on the other side of the curtain. Or maybe it's not so much that the curtain grows thin as that the light behind the curtain grows stronger, so that the shadows of unseen things become for the moment visible.

This wasn't the first time I'd been in such a place. Near the end of my childhood I had a glimpse of some of the truths that live behind the surface of things. It was in those thin places of my youth that I first turned away from the faith of my fathers.

Chapter II

Ready for Revolution

The faith of my father—and my mother—is mainstream Protestant Christianity, backed up by the kind of education that gets you a white-collar job or a white-collar spouse. It was the tension between these twin oaks of my home—applied faith and applied intellect—that started my spiral from Christianity as a young woman. It was that same tension that pulled the spiral back in my middle years, but in the beginning, when I was just a kid, that tension didn't exist. My roots were religion and education entwined; it never occurred to me that they could grow into separate trees.

Child of altar and blackboard

Shortly after World War II, my parents, Roger and Esther, met at Otterbein College, a small, church-affiliated liberal arts college near Columbus, Ohio. Both were preacher's kids—the children of Evangelical United Brethren ministers. (The E.U.B.'s merged with the Methodists in 1968, forming the current United Methodist Church.)

Roger had started his college education in 1942 but was drafted in the middle of his freshman year. When he returned to Otterbein in 1946, having fought in the Battle of the Bulge and served in the occupation of Europe, he knew exactly what he wanted to do with his life. He entered Otterbein's School of Education on the G.I. Bill and advanced steadily toward a degree. He met and fell in love with Esther Scott, the bright and beautiful Otterbein Winter Princess of

1947. Years later, my mother tried to describe to me how it felt, after living two years on a campus filled with women and a few men who were either 4-F or studying for the ministry, when the G.I.s came home at last.

"They looked so good," she said. "You just can't imagine. They looked so good."

Esther and Roger were married two days after Esther's graduation ceremonies in June of 1947. After Roger graduated the following year with a bachelor's in Education, he got a job in a small-town Ohio school system as a history teacher and a boys' sport coach. My sister, Rose, was born soon after, followed in the next few years by me and then my brother, Brian. The year I was born, Roger got a job teaching and coaching in a larger school system near Mansfield. By the time I was nine years old, he was superintendent of schools, and superintendent of our E.U.B. church's Sunday School, to boot.

On the one hand, I knew from Sunday School and from the religious education taught in the public schools in those days that God was the Supreme Being. On the other hand, God was neither here nor there when report cards came out. I could no more have gotten out of doing my homework by claiming a need to spend more time in prayer than by claiming a need to play poker with the boys. We worshiped equally at the dual altars of church and school in my home. Fortunately, I was good at both: one of the smart kids at school and an acolyte on Sunday mornings.

In a way, church was a better fit for me as a child than school. Throughout the elementary grades, I clung to my position as one of the smart kids on the strength of stand-out language skills, which were enough to make up for mediocrity in arithmetic and incompetence in non-academics such as art and physical education. I took comfort in the fact that I might produce buckets of bad art and fail at every attempt to throw, kick, hit, or catch a ball, and that I might be humiliated by these failures, but at least I was still smart.

Church offered no such challenges to my place as a favored child. I relished being an acolyte, not least because it gave me the opportunity to light a match all by myself in the privacy of the sacristy before the service started. Our church preferred young acolytes—I was probably about eight years old when I got the job—and it was the only match I was allowed to light all week. I used it to light the brass candle lighter's thick, paraffined wick, which fed out the end of a narrow spout by means of a small lever on the lighter's handle.

Lighting the match was great, but the best part of the job happened when I emerged from the sacristy door in my white robe, head held high, carrying the flaming candle lighter with its bell-shaped snuffer before me. I crossed to center stage and lighted the two candles at the altar while the whole congregation watched. I then exited stage right, blew out the flame, shed the tools of my trade, and went to Story Time. There I half-listened to Bible stories while watching the clock on the wall like a zealot. Fifty minutes later, I got to leave Story Time before anyone else, return to the place where I'd left my accouterments, pull on my robe, take up the candle lighter (this time unlit, and with the bell side forward), and reverse everything I'd done before, again in front of the whole congregation. After snuffing the candles, I exited stage left into the sacristy where I had started an hour earlier. A deeply satisfying ritual. It was always tempting to light another couple of matches back in the sacristy before meeting my parents outside the church doors to go home. Usually, I resisted the temptation. An acolyte who used up her matches too fast might lose her job.

Church let me be a star without the tension that went with stardom at school. When our church had a Children's Service, I was chosen to read the scripture lesson almost as a matter of course; I was the best reader among the kids and would have been stunned if anybody else was tapped for the job. After reading the lesson in a loud, clear voice with no hesitations or mistakes, I retired to a chair beside the altar, and the kid who got picked to read the morning prayer approached the lectern. He stumbled and mumbled his way through a prayer that one of the Sunday School teachers had written for him while I thought it was a pity I couldn't just do all the jobs myself.

Even after I was replaced by a younger acolyte, grew too old for Story Time, and had to sit with my parents through the grownup Sunday service, I was not unhappy at church. The first half of the service had some variety, with hymn-singing and readings. The second half—the sermon—was so boring I never left church with the slightest memory of any thought or sentence the preacher had uttered; still, there were ways to pass the time. I practiced moving my eyes in and out of focus, changing the two candles on the altar into four, then eight, then back to four, and back to two again. I leafed through the hymnal, reading over the words of my favorite hymns. : the gory ones.

Some were gory and solemn: *"In the old rugged cross, stained with blood so divine, a wondrous beauty I see . . ."* Others were gory and rousing: *"There is a fountain filled with blood, drawn from Emmanuel's veins; and sinners, plunged beneath that flood, lose all their guilty stains."* The idea of plunging into a blood-filled fountain and emerging cleaner than I went in held a stomach-turning fascination. I read those words over most every Sunday, imagining the blood closing over my head (Would it be warm or cold? Should I hold my nose or not?) and then dripping off me when I stepped out of the fountain, mysteriously clean and white as new-fallen snow.

When I hit puberty and had crushes on boys, I took a liking to the hymn "In the Garden," even though it wasn't gory. This hymn tells a story of walking out to a garden to be alone with Jesus: *"I come to the garden alone, while the dew is still on the roses."* I imagined that it wasn't Jesus, but the object of my current crush waiting for me in the garden: *". . . and he walks with me, and he talks with me, and he tells me I am his own, and the joy we share as we tarry there, none* other has ever known." Letting my imagination flow along those lines passed the time about as well as it could be passed in church.

Before emerging from childhood I was, finally, challenged in my relationship to God and Jesus, but it didn't happen in church. The summer after I turned twelve, my parents sent me to a week of a Christian church camp in West Virginia. At camp I had my first up-close experience with hell and redemption, which changed my relationship to Jesus and drew me temporarily closer to the church. And yet it was that same experience that sowed the seeds for my later desertion.

That's because I was saved at summer camp, and it was only after I was saved that I could know for certain I was going to hell.

Saved by Jesus and my mom

I enjoyed the drive to camp, sitting beside my mom in the front seat, just the two of us. The two-lane road cut through the Allegheny foothills, their convoluted strata ribboning up and down on either side of the family station wagon. My camp was located in a valley encircled by those hills. At the bottom of the gravel road that spilled into the campgrounds, teenagers stood in matching T-shirts holding clipboards. Mom stopped our car and said my name to one of the girls.

The girl looked at her clipboard, then pointed to a row of low buildings and said, "Bunkhouse C, Room 3." She looked through the car window at me. "Hi, there. Glad you could make it. Go inside and pick out a bunk. Put your suitcase on your bunk."

Mom drove around to the bunkhouse and helped me get my suitcase out of the back seat. She told me to have a good time, kissed me, and drove away.

Room 3 was at the end of the bunkhouse's one hallway. I looked in the open door. Light came from two mesh windows cut into the bare wooden walls. The only furnishings were six double-bunk beds, all empty. I was the first in my group to arrive.

I put down my suitcase and stood in the doorway, pondering. How do you pick out a bunk? Was one bunk better than another? A girl my age shoved past me, ran inside, slammed her suitcase on a lower bunk against the opposite wall, and yelled, "This one's mine!"

Was it better to be against a wall? Were lower bunks better?

Two girls came in together and nabbed upper bunks next to each other, one against a wall and the other in the middle of the room. They helped each other lift their suitcases up, then scrambled after them and began whispering across the gap between the bunks. When they saw me looking at them, they moved closer to the edge of their beds and lowered their whispers.

Campers poured around me and chose their bunks. I felt at the center of a vacuum, as if empty space had opened up around me. No one looked at me, and yet I was sure that everyone was aware I didn't know what to do. Finally, a teenage girl with a clipboard came in. "Does everybody have a bunk?" She saw me standing beside my suitcase. "Choose a bunk." she said.

It was as if I were nailed to the floor. My brain had stopped working. Finally, she pointed to the only empty bunk left, an upper in the middle of the room. "That one's yours."

I walked over and tried to heft my suitcase onto the bed's surface, but it was too heavy and I couldn't lift it over my head. The teenage girl—our counselor, it turned out—looked at the girl lying on the bunk below mine. "Help her," she said.

Rolling her eyes, the girl helped me shove my suitcase up. I said thanks, then climbed the ladder and toppled onto the gray blanket that covered my bunk, the worst bunk in the room, since it was the one that no one else wanted.

Our counselor handed out a schedule of activities for the week.

"Change into swimsuits," she said, "and then put your suitcases under your bunks. Keep your suitcase under your bunk at all times, except when you need to get something out of it."

Keep our suitcases *under* our bunks? In that case, why start by putting them on the bunks? I skimmed the sheet of activities for the week—swimming, crafts, softball, crafts, hiking, crafts. It dawned on me that camp consisted of physical education and art, my two worst subjects at school, alternating from dawn to dusk for a solid week. We had one hour a day to ourselves. It was to be spent in the bunkhouse, on our bunks.

"We leave for the pool in two minutes!" said our counselor. I opened my suitcase and rummaged for my swimsuit. I didn't want to get undressed in front of everybody, but couldn't see a way out.

If I was ever happy for a minute at summer camp, I don't remember that minute. I longed for home every day and cried in my pillow at night for the comfort of my own room, my own bed, my mother who loved me, the luxury of privacy, the affection of friends.

I didn't make a single friend in the compressed time of summer camp. Instead, there was the humiliation of trying to find a partner for those events that required one, of always asking a stranger because whoever was my partner yesterday had made a friend and no longer needed me today.

I wasn't kissed at summer camp, though I longed to be kissed, and formed a crush on an older boy camper before the end of the first campfire sing-a-long. But by sing-a-long the second day he had a girlfriend, deeply tanned, who could swim like a fish. She teased him at the pool about how skinny he was until he grabbed her towel and threw it in the wading pool, to screams of delight and outrage by other kids who, mysteriously, seemed to be their friends already.

Summer camp meant no privacy and no time to do what I wanted to do, which was read comic books. Instead, time passed with excruciating slowness in scheduled activities. We had daily inspections of bed and barracks. They inspected our teeth after we were up and dressed to be sure that we had brushed them. They sent us back to the communal bathroom if they weren't satisfied with what they saw. I was as miserable as I'd ever been.

On Friday night, the last night of summer church camp, all I could think about was the next morning when my mother would come to take me away from this terrible place. She would look at me with love. It would be the first time I'd seen such a look in seven days, and I was parched for it.

That Friday night the whole camp gathered on risers around a huge bonfire. I sat alone in the crowd watching the flames move and the sparks fly toward heaven. We sang a few hymns that everybody knew—"Jesus Loves Me," "This Little Light of Mine"—and then one of the counselors stood in the light of the fire and started to talk about Jesus. About the peace and joy of letting Jesus into our hearts. About going home tomorrow cleansed, ready to live a life without sin, a life with Jesus beside us as our friend every minute of every day.

The counselor asked if any of us had stories about Jesus in our lives. A few kids stood up and said something. I wanted to be one of them, but I couldn't think of anything to say. Together, we sang the spiritual "Kumbaya," its verses designed to pluck the heartstrings.

"Someone's praying, Lord," we sang in one verse. More than anything I needed this comfort, this simplicity in my life. I knew that I was a sinner. Longing for my mother, I remembered all the times I'd lied to her, disappointed her, made her angry or sad. My mother who loved me. How could I do that to her? If I let Jesus into my heart, he would help me live a life without such sins.

"Someone's crying, Lord," we sang, and that someone was me. Tears poured down my cheeks. The counselor asked if we were willing to let Jesus into our hearts. Those who were willing were called forward to join hands around the fire. I was the first one there. Sobbing, I promised to love Jesus. The counselor told us that we were washed clean of our sins and that we were to go forth and sin no more. I felt crystal clear, hollow, a perfect vessel for our Lord.

Solemnly I followed the dark path to the bunkhouses with the rest of the campers. This night, for once, I didn't care if anybody else wanted to talk over the day's events with me. I was one with Jesus and at peace. A rather weepy peace.

The next morning, Mom came with the other parents. With one look, I could see that she still loved me, and I offered a silent prayer of thanksgiving. On the drive home I was as good as gold, sinless. But that night when Mom asked if I'd brushed my teeth, I said "yes" even though the true answer was "no." She kissed me good night and left me alone with my lie. I asked Jesus to forgive me and help me, but he didn't seem as real as he had around the campfire.

The next day, thinking that maybe the flames and sparks of the bonfire had made me feel Jesus' presence, I stole a book of matches from the kitchen drawer and hid with them behind the tool shed. Stealing and playing with matches were more sins, but I told myself it was okay if they got me closer to Jesus. I crouched down and lit one of the matches. A breeze blew it out. I lit another match, and it blew out, too. In desperation, I used my third match to light all the others in the book at once. This time, the fire didn't go out. I stared into the sulfurous flames, trying to find Jesus. I didn't notice the shrinking match stubs until the fire was directly under my thumb and pain radiated from my hand throughout my body.

I struggled to keep from crying out loud—what if Mom heard me?—and dropped the flaming remains of the book on the grass. I stayed on my knees, choking with sobs, blowing on my seared thumb, until the matches burnt themselves out and I could control myself enough to safely emerge from behind the tool shed in sight of the kitchen.

My thumb didn't blister, though it did stay pink and tender for a couple of days. That night, noticing my air of gloom, Mom asked if anything was wrong, and I had to lie again and say I was fine. I didn't bother to ask Jesus for forgiveness this time. Even at my young age, I knew enough about redemption to know that I wasn't saved after all. I didn't actually regret my sins and would commit them again tomorrow if given half a chance, being more careful not to burn my thumb next time. I was a common and unrepentant sinner, and if there was a hell after this life, I was destined to reside in it for eternity.

I got "saved" three times before I turned fourteen: twice in Christian summer camps and the last time in front of my parents at a revival service. In matters of redemption I must have been a slow learner, because each time I believed myself to be washed clean of sin and committed to a life walking hand-in-hand with Jesus. At my final conversion, in the revival service, my mother looked into my tear-stained face with an expression I remember as being slightly removed, as if she saw a curio on a shelf rather than the pure, holy, washed-white-as-snow soul that I had suddenly become.

Being saved brought me temporarily closer to the trappings of religion. The first Sunday in church after each of my savings, I was especially attentive, especially holy. I didn't daydream about boys "In the Garden"; I just read my gory hymns over and over. But in the long run, being saved didn't unite me to God or the church. The contrary. As the years passed, I was embarrassed to remember my tears, and the manipulations that led to them made me cynical about organized religion.

Now I understand that I was operating under a very basic misunderstanding of what it means to be saved. Being saved doesn't mean being sinless from that time forward. Being saved doesn't shoot you straight to heaven or create an instant saint. What you're accepting is a path through the forest that you'll take again and again—not a one-time tornado ride to the Emerald City.

Saved by the insect world

The transformation I was ready for came from the other taproot of my family life—school. When I was thirteen we moved to Sidney, Ohio, a small city not far from Dayton. My father was superintendent of the city school system and chair of our church's building committee. At last the bad parts of school began to fall away and the good parts got better. In the eighth grade, arithmetic turned into algebra, then later into geometry. Released from the tedium of drilling multiplication and division tables, I fell in love with mathematics' mental gymnastics. It was also in the eighth grade that I created my last bad art in the final compulsory art class of our public school system. Things were looking up. In the ninth grade we took general science from Mrs. Harris, and I had a conversion experience there much more long-lasting and profound than any that had happened to me in church.

On the first day of ninth grade, Mrs. Harris offered extra credit to anyone who made an insect collection with a display case and scientific identifications. I liked insects, especially the iridescent and colored ones, so I took her up on it. I bought myself a little net at the hardware store and checked books out of the library for identification. That Saturday, following Mrs. Harris's instructions, I asked my mom for an empty mayonnaise jar, a bottle of ammonia, some cotton balls, and an empty cigar box. Out in our garage, I put the cotton balls in the bottom of the mayonnaise jar, soaked them in ammonia, fitted a piece of cardboard with holes punched in it over the cotton, and smashed the cardboard down to leave room for the insects. Then I looked around. A fly landed on the lid of one of our garbage cans. I clamped my mayonnaise jar over it. It flew into the jar and I closed the lid. I watched through the clear glass while, in the next few seconds, it died. I opened the jar, picked the fly out with a pair of tweezers, and impaled it with a sewing pin in my cigar-box display case. With the help of my Golden Nature Guide, I identified my specimen as a Housefly (*Musca domestica*). Then I went out after something a little more exciting.

In the half hour it took me to ride my bike from the corn and soy bean fields at Sidney's western border out to Tawawa Park at the eastern edge of town, I probably saw or heard at least a hundred species of insects. The fields supported a healthy army of giant spur-throated grasshoppers, and every lawn and garden in town whirred with their pygmy grasshopper cousins. Tawawa Park contained meadows of velvety mourning cloak butterflies, water striders skittering across the green surface of the fishing ponds, and dragonflies with wings that flashed all the colors of the rainbow.

Before I became an insect collector, I had never had the nerve to hold a spur-throated grasshopper in my hand, but with quiet cunning I'd often managed to capture a pygmy grasshopper, feel its legs and wings press against my closed palm, and finally release it, a smear of tobacco juice on my hand. Now, armed with my mayonnaise jar, I captured, killed, pinned, and identified both varieties on my first outing. In a matter of weeks, I had a tower of cigar boxes on my bedroom desk, each one filled with dead, labeled insects.

I enjoyed almost every aspect of insect collecting: catching insects in my net, closing them in the killing jar, watching them die, taking them out, pinning them in my cigar-box display cases, and identifying them. The only part I didn't like was making neat little labels. It reminded me too much of art.

I noticed that different kinds of insects died in ammonia gas at different rates. Delicate insects, like flies, crickets, and cabbage butterflies, died almost immediately. Honey bees took longer, and hornets and wasps the longest of all. I could catch a thread-waisted wasp, shut it in my lethal jar, and twenty minutes later it would still be struggling against the clear glass. I didn't like wasps as much as brightly colored insects, but I admired their black, sleek bodies, so like the evil queen in *Snow White*. Their fierce grasp of life won my respect.

Gradually, the joy drained out of insect collecting. The insects I loved the most, the bright butterflies and iridescent dragonflies and beetles, lost what I loved about them in the process. I learned to handle dead butterflies carefully, but even with all my care some of the colored dust that made them beautiful fell away. Pinned and labeled against the white typewriter paper that lined my cigar box, they presented a raggedy appearance, a disquieting contrast to their intense color and fragile perfection the moment before my net fell.

The subtle iridescence in dragonflies and beetles invariably faded to flat gray or black after a few days out of the sun. In time, I found myself averting my eyes from that part of the collection.

Even the sight of the wasp fighting for life in the killing jar began to make me uneasy.

Finally, I stopped collecting insects. I handed in my cigar box, got my extra credit, and threw away my killing jar. I still loved insects, even more now that I knew their names. I still tried to identify insects that were new to me. This was nowhere near as easy a task when I couldn't pin them down.

Today, I can look back on that year and see that collecting insects and then not collecting insects caused a conversion in me more profound and long-lasting than any that took place in church. At the time, it didn't feel like conversion: I didn't cry, and I didn't sense God at work in my cigar boxes. But I had walked through a door, and the world on the other side held more chances for the divine to show through.

Now, in late summer I stand among the flowers and earth and grass, surrounded by insects of all kinds: ants, bees, ladybugs, butterflies, earwigs. I watch them move, hear their wings beat the air.

A fat bumblebee grasps a yellow hawksbeard flower. The flower head gives against the bee's weight, bending halfway to the ground. The fat bumblebee almost covers the flower. The flower's narrow stem bounces under the bumblebee's weight. The bee slowly crawls over the flower head, back and forth, taking its time. Finally it lifts off, and the flower springs up. The bee alights on the next yellow hawksbeard flower, and the flower's head gives against the weight. Watching the bumblebee, I'm an innocent girl with a grasshopper on her open palm, and I'm a killer of thread-waisted wasps, and I'm the one who chooses not to kill this particular bumblebee because I love it alive more than dead.

Not only did collecting insects and then not collecting insects teach me about the natural world, it also changed the way I viewed my place in the universe. Choosing to kill insects taught me about insects; choosing not to kill them taught me about myself. It helped me connect my actions to their consequences. It made me more conscious. These are the sorts of things that religions sometimes claim to do—help us find our place in the universe, make us more conscious. In my teen years I found these things in the world of intellect, not the world of faith.

I was a good girl, obedient and respectful, so it took awhile for me to abandon the faith of my fathers. In fact, through high school what faith I had became more brittle, more absolute. For example, because Jesus never had any money, I insisted that our church's youth group never have any money in our bank account, either. If we ever did anything to raise money, I insisted that we spend it like Christians—that is, on people other than ourselves. Under my lash the youth group was a dour and cheerless lot, and I suspect they all breathed a sigh of relief when I finally graduated from high school, went off to college, and left them to spend what little money they raised on treats.

Once I hit college, the change came all at once. I read Mark Twain's hilarious, biting satires on religion, and whatever bubble of faith I retained for the literal truth of Bible stories exploded on contact with Twain's barbed wit. ("The Diary of Adam and Eve" and "Extract from Captain Stormfield's Visit to Heaven" are particularly wonderful.) Under the impression that I might be a great thinker, I signed up for Philosophy 101, only to spend the quarter bored to the edge of oblivion by the dense, cerebral writings of great thinkers of the past. The one bright spot of the course came in a single lecture during which our professor stood on a stage before an auditorium of underclass students and ran through an elegant proof that God could not be proved. At the end of that hour I stood up, breathed a sigh of relief, and it was all over. If God could not be proved, then what was the point? As far as I could tell, religion's only purposes were to distort the truth about the universe and my place in it, then try to get me to stop thinking so much. It seemed to me that religion's goals were in direct opposition to a good education. Religion and education—the intertwined roots of my childhood—were revealed as two separate, mutually incompatible beings, each poison to the other. I was surprised that my parents could live so peacefully with this contradiction.

I discovered the joy of sleeping in on Sunday mornings.

Regardless of my newfound understanding of the nature of things, I still had to go home for Thanksgiving break. I didn't have the moral fiber to announce over the turkey that I was no longer a member of the body of Christ, so on Sunday morning I dragged myself out of bed and went to church with my parents and sister and brother, just like always. My sister, Rose, and I went together to the young adult Sunday School class. The lesson was the story of Noah's flood. Our class leader insisted that the story be taken at face value. In the flood, God destroyed every living thing on the earth except Noah, his family, and a male and female member of every species of animal, who all lived together for forty days and forty nights on the ark, after which they dispersed and repopulated the land. That's what happened. What did it mean? He looked at me, maybe thinking he could welcome me into the group by including me in the discussion. "What do *you* think?" he asked.

"It couldn't have happened that way," I said, certain of the irrefutability of my argument. "There are more than eight million species of insects in the world. How did they all get on the ark?"

After a pause, the leader answered, "Maybe some of those insects evolved after the flood."

"*Evolved?*" A person who could hold the theory of evolution and a literal reading of Noah's flood in his brain at the same time was simply, in my opinion, not thinking clearly. "That's stupid," I announced. Then I sat in silence while the group continued their discussion around me.

Between church and Sunday dinner, Rose and I talked over the idiocy of the young adult Sunday School class, and between bites of my mother's Sunday pot roast, I screwed up my courage. Over ice cream dessert, I gave my parents an ultimatum. I was willing to join them for Sunday services since it meant so much to them to have the whole family together on the pew, and since I could just sit there without participating, but I would not attend Sunday School ever again. Confident that Rose was on my side, I said that if they couldn't live with that decision, my sister and I would both move out of home, get jobs and an apartment, and finance our own college education.

Rose said "Uhhhh, wait a minute," my father argued, my mother wept, but I won. Rose and I stopped going to Sunday School. Except for visits home or events such as weddings and funerals, I never attended services of any kind. After graduating from college, I stopped going to Sunday services at home, too, though my mother asked me at the start of every visit whether I was coming to church on Sunday, assuring me that I would be very, very welcome. Finally I structured my visits home so they didn't include a Sunday, just to avoid the question.

My breakup with religion felt like a great escape. I luxuriated in free Sunday mornings for years.

Ready for revolution

A quarter of a century passed—nearly a quarter of my life, if I live as long as my grandmothers did—before I began to feel a lack in the spiritual side of my life.

No single incident sparked this desire for change. It was an accumulation of small, everyday events. Maybe it wasn't the events themselves, but the growing sense of being trapped by them, of reliving my mistakes again and again without ever wising up. After graduating from college and then from graduate school, I held down a variety of jobs. I wrote poems and stories that a few people read; later, I wrote software manuals that many people owned and some read. As the years and experiences rolled by, I gradually grew aware of patterns in my life that I wanted to break, without knowing how.

It might be a forgiving that I couldn't offer. A harsh word I couldn't swallow, couldn't take back, and couldn't forget saying. I felt stalled in matters of blame and responsibility. I'd be fine for a while, cycling along the path of life, whistling and feeling like a competent human being, and then *wham*, someone stumbled across my path, we collided, and I fell into an emotional ditch, bruised, angry, and resentful. As the years passed I collected many memories of this ditch. After each new impact, as I tumbled down into it, I'd think, *Oh no, not again!* Yet I didn't seem to get much better at climbing out of the ditch.

I wanted to be kinder, but wanting to be kinder didn't make me more kind. I had begun to feel emotionally distant from people I cared about, and it seemed to me that the distance was growing. Would I turn into a dry husk of an old woman, human on the outside and nothing on the inside?

I became aware of an increasing sense of detachment from creation itself. Intellectually, I knew this to be a delusion. I could no more be detached from creation than I could be detached from my own DNA. Still, at times I felt cold, hard, and alone, like a piece of gravel thrown a million miles into empty space. Would I die feeling that way?

These didn't seem to be questions I could address with my intellect. In fact, as I observed how other people coped with these issues in their lives, it seemed possible that more I.Q. points could make my situation even worse.

The political problems I encountered when I joined the board of the writer's conference sent me careening to the edge of the ditch. I stayed near the edge through my term on the writer's board, even tumbled in a few times, and each time my "atheist's prayer" helped me crawl up and get going again. As a phenomenon, that prayer seemed to have a lot of potential, but I didn't know where to go with it. It was as if I'd gone fishing for the first time, caught a little shiner, thought *this is great*, and then tossed my line into the same pool again and again without catching anything else.

Writing these things down imposes a coherence on them that they didn't have at the time. As long as I worked for software companies, I was too busy to think about what was happening; I observed myself changing but didn't have the mental space to figure it out. After leaving the technical world, I wanted to figure it out but didn't know how to get started. I didn't think I could either come to a better understanding of the spiritual side of life or become a better person just by getting some books out of the library and taking good notes—my standard approach to a new problem. Thinking about it by myself wasn't getting me anywhere, either.

Besides, I didn't want to do it by myself. Many wise people have grappled with these issues over the millennia, and many wise people are grappling with them right now. It seemed stupid to stumble around in my individual mind, poking holes in fallacies that had already been ripped to tatters a thousand times before. I needed a team to work with me on this.

Where would I find it?

Chapter III

Dreadful Religion

Where could I find the right group of travelers for the next stage of my journey?

I could look for a church to join. I was raised in the church, so I knew that these issues came up beneath the stained-glass windows. People prayed in churches. They prayed together, they prayed separately, they prayed for each other. In addition to the prayer thing, I wanted help in living a "good" life. On any given Sunday morning, I knew that some aspect of goodness would be touched on in most churches. If I wanted help with these issues, why not join a church?

Because I knew them, that's why. After all, I was the granddaughter of two Christian ministers. "The Bible" had always been my favorite *Jeopardy* category because, unlike most *Jeopardy* contestants, I'd actually read it. I'd been saved, for Christ's sake, *three times*. You couldn't tell me about organized religion. I knew where those people came from. I'd been there and traveled on. How could they help me when I was beyond them?

I've been burned before . . .

My knowledge of religion filled me with misgivings. I disapproved of so much that seemed fundamental to the faith traditions of my culture, I doubted that I could ever be part of them.

I disapproved of the exclusiveness, the idea that "we" (whoever that is) have the one and only path to salvation, that we go to heaven and the rest of you poor schmucks roast in hell for eternity.

I disapproved of the obsession with historical events and linear time, reducing myth and metaphor to pseudo-facts, meaningless if they didn't occur in a particular time and place in history. The Flood makes a pretty good myth; as history, it seemed silly.

I disapproved of the overwhelming maleness of it all—the Father, the Son, Abraham, Peter, Paul. The absurdity of an all-male clergy. The masculine pronoun, and *only* the masculine pronoun, used to refer to God. To be female and a major character in the stories of faith from my childhood, it seemed as if you had to be all symbol and no authority. You either symbolized "the fall" like Eve or you symbolized purity like Mary, an ordinary girl forced into perpetual virginity so that she could embody some guy's ideal for female virtue.

My biggest problems with religion sprang from the Judeo-Christian tradition I was raised in. I was aware, of course, that I had other choices. There was Buddhism, Paganism, New Age. There was therapy. These and other options were available even in the small town on the edge of the Olympic Peninsula where David and I had moved. The contractor who set the tile in our new kitchen was a practicing Buddhist, friendly and willing to share information. The local women's center offered a moon circle ritual at each new moon. The newspaper's "Community Billboard" listed dream groups, mid-life-spiritual-tune-up groups, dance-and-drum groups.

But if I didn't trust the Christians, I was equally suspicious of everybody else. I had little faith in newly minted ritual and no interest in single-gender spirituality. Buddhism at least had the weight of millennia behind it without all the baggage Christianity had acquired, and yet, I suspected that any good, solid religious tradition would have its own sets of weighty luggage.

The way I saw it, across the board, organized religion displayed a depressing picture of personal and social corruption. The more successful the religion, the greater the corruption. Give any religion a few thousand years of solid growth, and what have you got? A rigid, pervasive institution that prescribes status and behavior, uses ritual for control rather than transformation, and loads an expensive, complacent bureaucracy on the financial backs of the very people that the institution claims to serve. How could I let any of these corrupt systems take charge of my spiritual life?

In addition to my disrespect for the institutions of religion, I was afraid of the loss of intellectual integrity that seemed an inescapable part of the religious life. Even religions that were relatively free of dogma tried to make some sense of a world that, as far as I could tell, didn't make sense. To embrace a religion, I was afraid that I'd either have to embrace a world view that contradicted my personal views, or be surrounded by it, clinging to my little island of rationality in a sea of rationalizations. I didn't see how I could do it.

. . . and I won't be burned again

And yet, I wanted to do it. I was like a bruised and cynical ex-wife, certain that all men were bastards and still longing for a good date—a date that could possibly lead to another. I stood at the entrance to the singles bar, afraid to walk through the swinging doors and afraid to stay out in the cold.

What got me moving was a memory of a couple of unpleasant events in my professional life that seemed to apply to the current dilemma. In the mid-1980s, I got laid off twice within a single year. As a result, I made a fundamental change in the way I viewed the relationship between me and an employer. If I applied the same change to the way I viewed the relationship between me and religion, maybe some of the problems would be easier to handle.

The first time I was laid off, it shocked me to the spine. I'd graduated from college with both a bachelor's and a master's degree in English Literature but no coherent career plan, so it had been a struggle to find my place in the working world. Finally, after a series of entry-level jobs, I wormed my way into the position of academic advisor at the branch campus of a small liberal arts college. I held that job for seven years and thought it was safe. Then the college administration wiped out the entire branch campus because it didn't fit in with their overall goals.

I needed my job to pay the rent and was hurt to learn that the college didn't think they needed me. But I couldn't do anything about it; I wasn't in charge. So I picked myself up, looked for other work, and eventually found it writing manuals for a small software company. A year later, my new employer laid off a third of its employees, including me, to meet its payroll. This time the shock didn't go quite so deep. I knew small software companies weren't the most reliable employers around. And besides, I still couldn't do anything about it; I wasn't in charge. So I picked myself up and started to look for work again. But now I had a new attitude.

After I was laid off the second time, I became unwilling to grant any employer that kind of control over my life ever again. For the next three years, I earned my living as a freelance technical writer, turning down all offers of employment. Even after I finally accepted a job at Microsoft, I entered into the relationship with a fundamental change in attitude. I kept the awareness that the alliance between me and my employer was a business partnership either of us could end at any time. The people who ran the company were in charge of setting the company's goals and making policy to achieve them. I was in charge of setting my professional goals and making policy to achieve those goals. Our partnership was the overlap between these two responsibilities.

I would do my best to help them put a computer on every desktop and in every home in the universe. In return, they would give me money and other things of material value, such as health insurance, a retirement plan, and company T-shirts.

I knew they still had more power in the relationship than I did. They could re-assign me, change my job duties, or lay me off, and there was little I could do about it. Though in theory I had similar powers—I could quit—my quitting would have much less impact on the organization than on me. But at least I no longer felt like the child in this relationship, helpless and hoping that the parent would take care of me. I was in a working partnership, and I knew I could take care of myself.

All I had to do, in looking for a church, was apply the same principles. The organization has its goals and I have mine. Is there any overlap? Can I contribute to the organization's goals and my own at the same time?

I knew these principles would be a lot harder to apply to a relationship with a church than with an employer. My initial relationship with the church had been established during childhood, and so the passive, parent-child aspects had had a chance to root themselves that much deeper. Also some churches actively encourage a parent-child relationship: they present the people who run the organization as parent figures; their clergy speak with parental authority from the pulpit; church employees and lay leaders claim that members owe the same kind of financial and emotional fealty to the organization that they owe their own families. However, not all churches are like that, and just because some presented themselves that way didn't mean I had to buy it.

Once I saw religion and the church in those terms, then the answer to the question, "How can I put them in charge of my spiritual life?" was obvious. *Don't.*

With this change in attitude, I found the courage to get off the cold sidewalk and walk through the swinging doors. In this way, I rationalized my return to church.

Chapter IV

Church Shopping

Each week in the local newspaper of my town, the "County Life" section prints a summary of the religious organizations in the area. They're listed in alphabetical order, from Bet Shira Congregation to Unity Center of Port Townsend. Once I decided to find a church, I sat at my dining room table, spread out the paper, and studied the listing—twenty-six organizations in all—with an open mind. When I was a kid, my family had always gone to Evangelical United Brethren churches, and then United Methodist churches, after the E.U.B.'s merged with the Methodists, so I didn't know that much about the other Christian denominations. I decided to give them all at least one shot at me. I would attend every religious organization in the area at least once before deciding where to focus my attention. It'd be broadening. It'd be educational. It'd also take half a year, but so what? I had the rest of my life to settle in.

Even though I was looking forward to being broadened, out of respect for my upbringing I decided to start with the Methodists, the denomination of my childhood. On a drizzly Sunday morning in early January, I climbed the worn steps to Trinity United Methodist Church in uptown Port Townsend. As I stepped into the small sanctuary, I felt an odd mixture of *deja vu* and *jamais vu*. Poinsettias from Christmas decorated the area around the altar, just as they had in my churches back in Ohio. And yet I was different, almost thirty years different, and to my eyes the poinsettias were from another universe. The church's stained glass windows included a small window of a sailing ship at sea. Having grown up in the Midwest, I'd never seen an image of a ship in a church window. I liked it.

This Sunday turned out to be the one nearest Epiphany, the celebration of the Magi's visitation to the infant Jesus and their recognition of his divinity. We sang "We Three Kings," one of my favorite hymns when I was a kid, especially that delectably gory fourth verse: *"Myrrh is mine; its bitter perfume breathes a life of gathering gloom; sorrowing, sighing, bleeding, dying, sealed in the stone-cold tomb."* The organist wore a nose ring, an ornament I hadn't seen before in church. She looked like she was about my age, mid-forties. We were the youngest people in the room by ten years or more. The tiny congregation—fewer than twenty people—was led by a woman minister, a retired elementary school teacher. During her Epiphany sermon, I was transported back to the second grade, sitting in the midst of surreally elderly classmates.

In spite of the sailing ship in the window and the organist's nose ring, I felt caught in a time warp to the 1960s—*my* 1960s. The familiar Methodist order of service, the poinsettias behind the altar, even the smell of old wood and damp plaster evoked my childhood, or more accurately, a part of childhood that I had deliberately left behind. I sat on my pew feeling callow and confined. When the service was finished, every member of the congregation shook my hand and said how much they'd like to see me again. I heard the voice of my mother asking again and again whether I would return to church to sit beside her on the pew. With as much grace as I could muster, I accepted their kind words, then escaped into the cold drizzle, knowing I wouldn't be back.

Too close to home.

Next, I tried the Presbyterians. The congregation was larger than at the Methodist church and included a children's class that sang a song for us at the start of the service. The kids were cute in their suits and starched dresses. They reminded me of how rarely I was with children, and that one advantage of joining a church might be the chance to spend more time with kids. The minister was a man about my age. He seemed comfortable with his audience and they with him. He preached the first of what he said would be four sermons on the question, "Who Was Jesus?"

It's a good question and one I was willing to hear addressed, but not the way he did it. He said he wanted to figure out who Jesus was from a historical perspective, but his only source was Holy Scripture, a notoriously unhistorical document. For an unbeliever like me, he stuck too close to the party line and sounded too much like he thought he knew what he was talking about. He also spoke too long, filling a half hour. I couldn't see myself sitting still for that on a regular basis.

The next week I dropped in on a fundamentalist service in a nearby town and nearly walked out during the morning prayer. In the guise of addressing God, the pastor scolded his congregation for their week's transgressions and then told them how to behave in the future. Within minutes, I was furious with him and everything coming out of his mouth. In his sermon, he informed us what God and Jesus expected of us with a rock-hard certainty that, to me, undermined every word he said. I could hardly wait to get out of there.

That Sunday afternoon, sitting at my dining room table with the list of churches I still hadn't attended in front of me, I felt my heart sink. Only three down, and if the rest were anything like those three, the next six months looked bleak. "This isn't going to work," I thought, "I'm not going to find one I like." It was like dating after a bad divorce and realizing that the horror stories you'd been hearing from your single friends were true—they were all jerks out there.

I knew my problems finding a church had to do as much with my attitude as it did with the particular churches I visited. Other people in the fundamentalist congregation didn't seem to mind being scolded during morning prayer, and at the Presbyterian church it took ten minutes just to get out afterward because of the press of people who wanted to talk over the preacher's answer to the question, "Who was Jesus?" I tried to figure out why I disliked those services so much. It wasn't that I expected to agree with everything I heard in church ... but I hated feeling as if I were being preached at. Maybe I was too uncertain of my own beliefs to tolerate a high degree of certainty from the pulpit. Whatever the reason, it wasn't working out.

I'd intended to go to all the Protestant Christian churches first, but now the weeks ahead of Lutherans, Baptists (four flavors within driving distance), Congregationalists, Seventh-Day Adventists, Church of Christ, Assembly of God, and on and on, seemed endless and pointless. Was it time to leave that mighty Protestant River and drop in on the Catholics, Jews, and Buddhists?

Just asking the question set off an internal alarm. Like it or not, my spiritual roots were in the Protestant Christian church. Even thinking about grafting myself onto a different tradition produced a feeling of intense loneliness. Before taking such a drastic step, I decided to give two more local denominations a chance: the Episcopalians, who seemed sort of like Catholics without the Pope; and the Unitarians, whom I didn't know much about. Our neighbors down the lane were Unitarians, and I liked them. They had invited me to their church, so I figured "why not!"

On two successive Sundays in February, I visited the Episcopalians and the Unitarians, and my prospects for finding a church started to improve.

A little redemption

I first stepped through the red arched doors of St. Paul's Episcopal Church on a Sunday morning during Lent. A gray-suited man with a thin face and wispy gray hair greeted me and handed me the week's order of service. In the small sanctuary, dark fir vaulting

reached skyward to the peak of the sloped ceiling. A single aisle between two rows of pews pointed to the altar where something was hidden under embroidered linen. Behind the altar, an arched,
stained-glass window glowed with color.

St. Paul's window depicts Christ seated with a youth kneeling at
his feet, the youth's head and arms on Christ's lap, Christ's arm
around the youth's shoulders. It's a clear, graphic rendering of spiritual solace. Within seconds of seeing that window, I was in tears. I
slipped into an empty pew and dug out a handkerchief. The only
sounds were the organ's prelude and the quiet rustling of people en-
tering the church, kneeling in private prayer, and settling into their
seats. After the prelude ended, a silence fell. Then the organ boomed
out the first notes of the opening hymn, everybody stood up, and a
procession of acolyte, priest, and choir, all robed from collars to
Keds, flowed down the aisle to the chancel. Classic theater.

Throughout the service—the scripture lessons, hymns, responsive prayers—I continued to feel the same thrill that live theater
evokes, except now I was in the play as well as attending it. For the
first time in years, I recited the confession, saying out loud that I had
left undone things that were right and done things that were wrong.
As the words formed on my tongue, a weight in my chest shifted and
rolled aside, leaving—what? Empty space behind? I was amazed
and puzzled at how much these words needed to be said.

After the scripture lessons were read, the parish rector stepped
up to the pulpit to deliver his sermon. He started by announcing that
for Lent this year, he had chosen to give up making sarcastic remarks
to people. The issue struck a nerve: a wave of titters, shuffles, and
mutters flowed through the congregation. He admitted that he found
giving up these remarks difficult and that he had already failed in his
resolve more than once. However, in struggling not to say what was
on the tip of his tongue, he had discovered something surprising.
When he succeeded in swallowing a sarcastic remark, he became

aware of an unresolved problem he had with the person he was talking to. After that happened a few times, he began to suspect that he
used his habitual sarcasm as a diversion from problems it would be
better to face. So, without his diversion, this Lent he found himself
forced to deal with interpersonal problems that he might otherwise
have avoided. He thought this was a good thing, even a godly thing.

Less than fifteen minutes after he'd started talking, the sermon
was over, and he invited us to all stand and say the Nicene Creed together.

While the rest of the congregation recited the creed around
me, I stood and thought about what I'd just heard. A man of God
who didn't tell me what God wanted me to do, but instead tried to
share something of his own stumbling path. The sermon was plainly
written and delivered, short and to the point. I felt that I could sit still
for that sort of thing again.

My first Episcopal service left me with a paradox. All the problems with doctrine that came between me and redemption when I was
eighteen were still there. In fact, you can hardly turn around in an
Episcopal service without bumping into the Father, the Son, the Holy
Ghost, or the Virgin. Since I wasn't sure how Episcopalians felt about
a confirmed doubter at the altar, I skipped communion.

And yet, somehow, I got a little redemption.

King Midas and the mind-body problem

The following week I was tempted to return to St. Paul's, but decided to complete my intended circle of candidates first and check
out the Unitarians. My Unitarian neighbors had told me that theirs
was a church without doctrine, which sounded promising after the
push-pull I felt in the Episcopal service. Maybe I could get in touch
with the sacred without actually having to believe in anything.

At that time, the Quimper Unitarian Universalist Fellowship met at a local community center. When I walked into the center's meeting room—a plain, rectangular space with acoustic tile ceiling and indirect fluorescent lighting—members of the fellowship were taking down tables from someone else's Saturday night bingo party and setting up chairs for the service. A woman with bobbed gray-brown hair and intelligent gray-brown eyes greeted me, made introductions, asked if I'd ever been to a Unitarian service before, and rustled me up a pamphlet titled "We Are Unitarian Universalists." Before I knew it, I was lugging tables, setting up chairs, and distributing hymnals. Meanwhile, the room gradually filled with chatting Unitarians.

What is it, when you first meet a group of people you don't know, that makes you recognize your own tribe? A thousand little things: clothes; hair styles; glasses per capita; the smell or lack of nicotine in the air; the tone of voice in conversations you can't quite overhear; what the first person who speaks to you says; whether anyone else speaks to you at all.

I couldn't name any one thing that told me I'd stumbled into an enclave of my own people, but I knew it before the last folding chair unfolded. I looked around the room and guessed that ninety percent or more of the adults around me had attended college. I could have been back at a faculty party in graduate school.

When the last chair was in place, everybody sat down, and—boom—the service started. There wasn't a vestment in sight. A woman in a flowered top and denim skirt lighted a candle in a chalice and read a few opening words. A woman in a white shirt, paisley vest, and chinos read the story of King Midas for the children. We sang hymns with familiar melodies and unfamiliar words: no Fathers, Sons, Ghosts, or Virgins here. We shared some joys and concerns, collected an offering, and settled in for the sermon. This turned out to be a thoughtful, twenty-five-minute discourse on that classic spiritual question: Is the mind *part* of the body, or is it *separate* from the body? A member of the congregation, the first *man* to take part in the service, delivered the talk. No definitive conclusions were reached. After he finished, the woman in the flowered top thanked him, read a few closing words, and blew out the chalice candle. Everybody stood up and moved toward the coffee urns behind the rows of chairs. The room bubbled with conversation.

I hadn't thought much about the mind-body problem since Philosophy 101 and was surprised to run into it at the heart of a Sunday service. It was also surprising to sit through a church service without having God mentioned once. A relief, of course, to someone who didn't know what she meant by God. Also oddly deflating. Still, I met some interesting people. I'd recently moved to Port Townsend, was looking for friends, and thought this crowd had possibilities. They struck me as a bunch of over-educated thinkers who liked to talk about ideas. Not snotty—they could listen as well as talk. They reminded me of ... of me, frankly. The earth may not have moved for me that Sunday, but it takes longer in some relationships than in others, and I thought I might come back, just to get to know those people better.

What is attractive?

That Sunday afternoon, I sat at my dining room table with the Unitarian order of service and an old copy of the Methodist hymnal that I'd kept with me ever since I left home so many years ago.

On the back of the Unitarian order of service were printed the Seven Principles of the Unitarian Universalist Church. I read them over and thought, "*Fine.* No serious problem with anything here." At some point I might want clarification on Item VI, where it talks about the goal of "world community." (We Unitarians aren't planning to

---

The Seven Principles
of the Unitarian Universalist Association

We, the member congregations of the Unitarian Universalist Association, covenant to affirm and promote:

I   The inherent worth and dignity of every person;
II   Justice, equity and compassion in human relations;
III Acceptance of one another and encouragement to spiritual growth in our congregations;
IV   A free and responsible search for truth and meaning;
V   The right of conscience and the use of the democratic process within our congregations and in society at large;
VI   The goal of world community with peace, liberty and justice for all;
VII Respect for the interdependent web of all existence of which we are a part.

From *Singing the Living Tradition,* published by Beacon Press, Boston; © 1993 by the Unitarian Universalist Association.

---

take over the world, right?) But with that clarification, I could wholeheartedly sign up for the whole program.

At St. Paul's the previous week, I had listened while the congregation recited the Nicene Creed from the Episcopal *Book of Common Prayer.* Because the Creed is used in most Christian churches, I thought it might be in my Methodist hymnal, and sure enough, I found it near the end of the readings in the back. I studied its words with the same feeling I'd had when I heard them recited around me the week before.

Hitting the Nicene Creed in the Episcopal service was like running into a basilica wall. There it was, all laid out, everything I didn't believe. I didn't believe that God was a father, a son, a ghost, or an amalgamation of the three. I didn't think that Jesus' mom was technically a virgin; I didn't think that Christian baptism was the only way

The Nicene Creed

We believe in one God,
   the Father, the Almighty,
   maker of heaven and earth,
   of all that is, seen and unseen.
We believe in one Lord, Jesus Christ,
   the only Son of God,
   eternally begotten of the Father
   God from God, Light from Light,
   true God from true God,
   begotten, not made,
   of one Being with the Father.
   Through him all things were made.
For us and for our salvation
   he came down from heaven:
by the power of the Holy Spirit
   he became incarnate from the Virgin Mary,
   and was made man.
For our sake he was crucified under Pontius Pilate;
   he suffered death and was buried.
   On the third day he rose again
     in accordance with the Scriptures;
   he ascended into heaven
     and is seated at the right hand of the Father.
He will come again in glory to judge the living and the dead,
   and his kingdom will have no end.
We believe in the Holy Spirit, the Lord, the giver of life,
   who proceeds from the Father and the Son.
   With the Father and the Son he is worshipped and glorified.
   He has spoken through the Prophets.
   We believe in one holy catholic and apostolic Church.
   We acknowledge one baptism for the forgiveness of sins.
   We look for the resurrection of the dead,
     and the life of the world to come. Amen.

From The Book of Common Prayer, published by The Church Hymnal Corporation, New York.

to get your sins forgiven; I didn't believe that I'd exist as myself after I died; and I found the whole idea of the physical resurrection blasphemous.

And yet . . . I wondered, as I read the words over and over, if I really knew what they meant. The Unitarian Universalist principles were obviously written with great care to be *clear*. They didn't offer up much in the way of interpretation. The language was plain and non-metaphoric right up to "the interdependent web of all existence," a metaphor not given to much variation in interpretations, anyway.

What a stunning contrast the language of the Nicene Creed presented: *"God from God, Light from Light, true God from true God, begotten, not made, of one Being with the Father."* Now what in heaven did *that* mean? Why make the point *"begotten, not made"*? The writers had something in mind there. What was it? I had no idea.

I understood the Unitarian principles with one reading and agreed with them. In contrast, I disagreed with every word in the Nicene Creed and wasn't sure I knew what it was talking about in the first place. But I was curious. Was St. Paul's a place where I could find out without getting anything rammed down my throat? People in the congregation had greeted me after church, and I had liked them. They didn't strike me as throat-rammers. I remembered the beauty of the service, the quirky sermon, the feeling of sorrow and relief that washed through me when I confessed myself to be a sinner and asked . . . whatever it was . . . for mercy.

I was attracted to the Unitarians because of the ways they were like me: in background, attitude toward organized religion, and reliance on process rather than doctrine. I *liked* it that their principles were clear. I have a lot of respect for clarity.

I was attracted to the Episcopalians for the sensuality and beauty of the service, and surprisingly, for the desire to argue with them about doctrine—the way they were *unlike* me.

I closed my Methodist hymnal. Next week, I thought, I'll go back to St. Paul's. And the week after that, maybe I'll try the Unitarians again. Then we'll see.

Six months later, I was a full-fledged member of both churches.

Chapter V

Getting to Know You

On the first and third Sunday of each month, I was an Episcopalian. At St. Paul's I knelt before the altar, asked forgiveness, promised to do my best to forgive others, and ingested the body and blood of the living Christ. I often cried.

On the second and fourth Sunday of each month, I was a Unitarian. At the Quimper Unitarian Universalist Fellowship, I listened to the children's story, lighted a candle to share a joy or concern, attended to the sermon, and ingested coffee and cookies during the discussion period. I often cried.

On the fifth Sunday, when there was one, I rested.

At each service, I got something I wanted and missed something from the week before. Gradually I became more involved in each church. St. Paul's sponsors a soup kitchen at a local teen hangout, and I cooked up some soup and served it to the kids. The Quimper Unitarian Fellowship decided to build its own church with volunteer labor, and I painted some door jambs. My problem with doctrine didn't go away, but it did evolve. The problem of doctrine turned out to be one of the main attractions that kept me coming back to both churches.

Getting to know the Episcopalians

After attending St. Paul's for a few Sundays, I found myself still drawn to the experience of the service and still at a loss on the doctrine thing, so I called up St. Paul's rector, Father Mark Taylor, and made an appointment. I would have made a similar contact at my Unitarian fellowship, but the Quimper Fellowship, smaller and younger than St. Paul's, was just at the point of hiring its first part-time minister and had no one for me to contact.

Lent had come and gone when I arrived at the door to Father Taylor's office, so I wondered if he was now free to make all the sarcastic remarks he wanted. Would he greet me with a stream of biting wit? Nothing like that happened. Instead, he invited me in, motioned to a chair next to his desk, then sat himself and waited for me to start talking. He wore a black shirt and clerical collar under a gray tweed sports jacket. The office contained a wall of bookshelves, a desk flanked by filing cabinets, and a wall for art—a driftwood cross, a painting of a butterfly, an odd drawing of St. Paul's church building rendered in a primitive style.

Not having much experience with priests, I began by saying that I was raised in churches with "pastors" and asked what he wanted me to call him. He said "Mark" was fine. If I didn't like that, "Father Taylor" worked, too. He wasn't crazy about "Father Mark." Neither was I, so that was okay.

Before our meeting, I'd sent Father Taylor—Mark, from now on—a letter explaining where I was in relation to Christian doctrine. That is, up in the air. Now I asked if I had to sign up for the whole program before taking communion. He said that practically nobody buys every article of Christian doctrine, and he didn't find it useful to try to calculate the exact percentage of belief required to get you into the fold. He told me that Episcopalians believed in the "real presence" of God in the communion sacrament but didn't go in for technical definitions of what that meant. He asked if I'd been baptized (yes, as an infant), then gave me three things: a *Book of Common Prayer*, a paperback entitled *Introduction to the Episcopal Faith*, and the advice to go ahead and take communion if I wanted to. He said he'd be happy to do what he could to help me on my spiritual journey. A few weeks later, he proved it by calling me up and inviting me to join a spiritual support group he was starting in his home.

When I heard Mark inviting me to a support group with other people from St. Paul's, the answer "No, thanks" came to my lips so fast I had to swallow and stutter around for a minute to give myself a chance to think about it. I don't like to go out to meetings. Also, I wasn't sure I wanted to hear about other people's problems; I was afraid that whatever spiritual support I offered would be thin and forced. In addition, I was afraid to be in a room with a bunch of Christians who all believed the same thing and thought I was one of them. I didn't want to be the oddball: to have to choose between alienating everybody by keeping my mouth shut or alienating everybody by saying I thought their faith was based on fairy tales. On the opposite end of that fear was the fear that I might become too Christian. About a month previously, in mid-June, my Unitarian fellowship broke up for the summer, and we wouldn't hold services again until school started in the fall. My fellow Unitarians told me this wasn't unusual in Unitarian churches. I liked the balancing act between my two churches and was afraid that if I attended only Episcopal services for the summer and also joined a weekly Episcopal discussion group, I might lose my balance and fall completely into the Christian sheep corral, never to be heard from again.

However, after telling Mark in his office that I was looking for help on my spiritual journey, it would be churlish to say no to his invitation just because of those fears. So I reminded myself that I was still in charge of my spiritual life, and that nobody could shove me off-balance without my own willing desire to fall. Then I said yes, I would join his group.

That first night in Mark's living room, we went around the circle introducing ourselves and saying what brought us here. Mark went first, confessing to a lifelong ambivalence about his calling and saying that he needed support in making decisions about his future. Then there was David, in the middle of his first year on the local vestry, the governing body at St. Paul's. He found running the church a spiritually draining experience and was trying to figure out why he even attended church anymore. Next in the circle came Barbara, a former vestry member who never attended church anymore, partially because of her earlier involvement in vestry. She said her observation of the world made it impossible for her to continue to have faith in a loving, all-powerful God who was active in the universe. Then there was Janet, a local schoolteacher seeking spiritual support after the death of her son by AIDS. Next came Ron, who explained that though he had been born in a secular family, he'd never felt spiritually at home there, sensing since he was an adolescent that he was really a Christian. Now he attended both St. Paul's and the local Russian Orthodox church, as well as participating in the odd pagan ritual. He'd been baptized as an adult at St. Paul's, but he told us that his true baptism had been self-administered, stark naked, total immersion, alone in a wilderness river.

Then came me, feeling nowhere near as odd as I'd feared. I stumbled through my introduction, telling how I'd been raised a Christian, left the church, and was back now with many doubts. I knew that even though I wasn't exactly *like* any of these other people, I didn't have to worry that they all believed the same thing and thought I did, too. My revelation was more about me than them. Because I grew up with practicing Christians, I thought I knew what they thought. In fact, I thought I knew more than they did, because I'd left them behind. But in one short hour this group of Episcopalians had made it clear that I didn't know them after all. We were all in different places, but that wasn't the same as saying that one of us was "ahead." And we were all in the same place—Mark's living room—trying to figure out where to go from here. I thought that possibly, just possibly, I could get something out of traveling with these people for a time.

One Wednesday night a week or two later, I was prattling on to the group about Jesus, and how I didn't believe in the miracles, the virgin birth, the resurrection, and how I didn't know if I could belong to a Christian church under those circumstances, when David, the new vestry member, gently suggested that I just "not worry so much about Jesus." The other members of the group quickly agreed. The essence of Christianity to him, he said, was grace: that grace was available all the time, to all of us. Again little murmurs of agreement around the circle.

It felt strange to have a member of the governing body of a Christian church tell me not to worry so much about Jesus. Strangely relaxing.

And so we met every week through the summer and into the fall. We had an informal agenda for the meetings: we started with a prayer, then went around the room telling what happened to us during the past week and speculating on how God might be at work in those events.

I was at ground zero in my ideas about what God was and how God worked—I didn't have the slightest idea—so I sometimes felt out of step with the process. But I quickly grew to like all the group members, with one exception. From the beginning, I couldn't figure out how I felt about Janet, the elementary school teacher. At our first meeting Janet said that she needed support in her grieving process for her only son. She told us this in a clipped, unemotional voice that set the tone for everything else she said in the weeks ahead.

It wasn't that Janet didn't want to tell about her week or didn't think she knew when God took a hand in it. It was that I could never figure out how she *felt* about what happened to her. It all seemed so mechanical. She skimmed the surface and never found any meaning other than the easiest and least threatening. Some kid in her class skinned his knee, she bandaged him up even though she was on a break, he was grateful and started paying more attention to her in class, and she figured that was God at work. Who would argue with that? Or care to?

After our first meeting, Janet rarely mentioned her son or his death, but just stuck to the events of the past week like a terrier to a T-bone. Some of the other group members and I started to question her about how she felt about what she was telling us. Each week, she deftly side-stepped our questions. This annoyed me. In fact, during her interminable recitations of the week's events, I wanted to shove her off the nearest cliff.

At other times, I found Janet the most endearing member of the group. One night, someone in the circle mentioned that when he was a kid, his father had told him that he had no sense of humor. The next week Janet brought him a cartoon she'd clipped about somebody who couldn't get a joke. It was a dumb cartoon, not very funny, but it made the man with "no sense of humor" smile. After that, every week Janet brought cartoons and magazine ads and handed them out to us, different ones for different people. A couple of times she brought me cartoons about being a writer: Snoopy typing on the roof of his dog house, or Calvin getting a "D-minus-minus" on a paper at school. They were silly cartoons, and yet I got a charge out of it when she brought one for me. Then she'd launch into her mechanical rendition of God at work in her past week, and I'd get all annoyed with her again.

One night after we'd been meeting for some weeks, Janet started her turn by saying she had made a special expedition the previous weekend. She, her husband and daughter, and a small group of close friends had sailed her late son's sailboat up to the San Juan Islands, carrying his ashes with them. The purpose of the trip was to scatter the ashes in passages between the islands. Janet told us who was there and how they took turns scattering handfuls of ashes, some standing apart at the rail and others grouped together near the bow.

During her recitation, I felt tension mounting inside me. Finally, Janet was talking about her son's death, but she might as well have been reciting her grocery list for all the emotion in her words. We heard in great detail how the car pools to the boat's moorage got arranged, but nothing about what I wanted to know. Did she get a feeling of closure from the experience? Was she glad the others were there, or did she wish she were alone? What really happened? Not a clue. Finally, I asked Janet how she felt about the trip. She straightened up in her chair, nodded, and said it was successful. She mentioned that at times the straits were completely enveloped in dense fog, so that they could see only a few feet of water around them and nothing of the islands. In her prim teacher's voice, she said that was "really neat."

Really neat? I gritted my teeth. Last week, Janet had found two quarters on the sidewalk near her home, and that was "really neat." This week, she scattered her son's ashes between islands in a dense fog, and that was also "really neat." I wanted to shake her, but shaking Janet didn't seem like the best way to help her deal with her grief—if grief was what she was feeling, which I frankly didn't know. In fact, I couldn't think of a helpful response. I let it pass. She described how everybody who went with them on the boat came back to her house for a potluck. She enumerated what dish each person brought and in what order they sat around the table. Then she was through and somebody else started to tell about his week.

At home that night, I showered and washed my hair, then sat on the edge of my bed with the blow dryer. It takes awhile to dry my hair, which is coarse and thick. As I bent my neck and aimed the hot air, I tried to think what I could do about Janet. She was driving me nuts, and one of these nights I'd say something to her that I would regret. We were supposed to support and help each other, but how do you help someone who never shows you how she feels? Maybe being a teacher had trained her not to show her deeper emotions. After all, she could hardly spill her guts to the eight-year-olds during show-and-tell. Part of me wondered if she even had deeper emotions. What if I just questioned her and questioned her until she either said something meaningful or quit the group? Would that help?

I sat on the edge of the bed, blew hot air at my head, and stewed. Then I had what I can only describe as a moment of grace. I suddenly caught a glimpse of myself from outside and above.

I saw Margaret trying to decide, under her blow dryer, what was wrong with Janet and what was needed to fix her. Once Margaret figured it out, she'd take on the job of getting Janet to do what she should do.

It was not a pretty sight.

Look, Margaret, I said to myself. *You aren't Janet's shrink, her priest, or her mother. Try a little humility here. Your role in the group is to listen and be supportive. That's the whole story. Get into your part and stop trying to play God.*

I turned off the dryer to let my hair cool for a minute. It was about halfway dry. I pictured myself, week after week, listening to Janet tell her events. I pictured myself smiling and nodding at her. Since I didn't know how she felt about anything, I couldn't say things like "Oh, no!" or "Gee, that's great!" All I could do was smile and nod.

That couldn't be right. Whatever my role in the group was, it was not to nod mindlessly at Janet week after week. There had to be another way. I bowed my head and turned on the blow dryer again.

Okay, I thought, this is a Christian group. Suppose we try looking at the problem from a Christian point of view. Jesus says we're supposed to love God with all our hearts and to love our neighbors as ourselves. If we manage these two things, we're doing okay. So, from a Christian standpoint, the solution is simple: love Janet. I didn't find this woman particularly easy to love, but it was my job to love her. How would I do that?

I had no idea what loving Janet meant in this context. Did it mean I was supposed to feel some emotion? Pity? The urge to nurture? I couldn't believe it was my Christian duty to whip up some emotional response to Janet's situation. Surely, in this context, "love" did not refer to an emotion, but to behavior. But *what* behavior?

Could the phrase *"God is love"* help me? It's one of those abstract religious statements that is hard to pin down, but I told myself to take it for what it was worth and try to advance the ball a few yards down the field. If God is love, what is the nature of love?

The first image I got was of that personal God who looks down from heaven and feels things about you all the time: empathizes with your problems, is sad or angry when you screw up, is proud when you do the right thing, wants you to be happy. I couldn't get into it. It felt too much like I was creating God in my image, or more accurately, in my mom's image. I told myself to forget about love as *emotion*. Think of love as *behavior*.

Take it for granted, I told myself, just for now, that God is love and also that God is the force of creation. In that case, the world—the world as it *really* is, not some pink-cloud world—must have something to teach me. But the world is so big and complicated that my mind kept sliding off in confusion. Finally, I decided to choose one thing to focus on. Something fundamental, inert, and unchanging. The first thing that popped in my head was a rock. Rocks left by glaciers litter the ground near my house, from pea-sized gravel to boulders. Okay. If God is love, and God made rocks, then the nature of a rock should tell me something about the nature of love.

What is the nature of a rock?

Well, first of all, I realized, it's not inert and unchanging. Rocks rise up from the earth. They get crushed and ground and dropped by glaciers. Lichens grow on them, or water freezes and cracks them, or I pick them up, polish them in my tumbler, and use them as decoration in my garden. A rock might seem inert when compared to the frenzy of living beings, but when I tried to see a rock from a cosmic eye—from God's eye—it was neither simple, inert, nor unchanging.

The picture was getting too complicated again. Erosion had distracted me. I put rocks aside and cast around for something else to illustrate the love of God.

How about stars? For eons, humans have sat under the night sky, looked up at the stars, and even associated the stars with God. The earliest people charted the skies and spun tales about the eternal constellations.

Except, I reminded myself, that constellations are no more eternal and unchanging than rocks. Our own sun was born and will die. We're made of the same material as stars. The atoms in us were once in stars and may be in stars again.

This was getting interesting.

Instead of casting about in my mind for the one thing in the real world I could use to discover the nature of God's love, I started to make a list of things in the real world. I focused on each item in the list, just the way it was. For each item, the first image that came to mind involved change. As part of its essential nature, each item on my list was transforming into something else. The list came in the form of a prayer and ended with the questions I was trying to answer.

> *Dear God, who made the rocks just the way they are,*
> *rising from the earth;*
> *Who made the stars just the way they are,*
> *red stars dying and new stars being born;*
> *Who made the wind just the way it is,*
> *bending a tree or breaking it;*
> *Who made the waters just the way they are,*

cold soup running with live ingredients;
Who made the mule deer just the way it is,
stepping from forest shade into meadow light;
Who made the gray mole just the way it is,
digging deep;
Who made us, who made me, just the way I am,
blood-filled and trembling, trying to move:

How do I love myself with your love?
Speak to me now, I beseech you.
How do I love others with your love?
Speak to me now, I beseech you.
How do I love You with your love?
Speak to me now, I beseech you.

Amen.

The next morning I typed my prayer into my computer. As I read it over, I remembered Janet passing out those dumb cartoons at the start of our sessions and how pleased I was when she brought one for me. Wasn't she doing what I struggled to do the night before? I had tried to see the world the way it really was. When she clipped those cartoons, Janet tried to see us the way we really were. The cartoons didn't judge us or try to fix us—they simply reflected what Janet saw. Was I capable of doing as much? When I looked at Janet, what did I see? I saw a mystery. Could I live with that?

I wrote a short note to Janet saying that I liked those little cartoons she gave me because they made me feel she saw me as an individual. I also said that I found her rather mysterious, and that I felt that I knew everyone else in our group better than I knew her. I said that this prayer came to me while I was thinking about her, so I sent it to her in the same spirit that she brought those cartoons to me.

I printed out the prayer and the note, stuck them in an envelope, and mailed them to Janet that day.

Now it would be great if I could say that at our next meeting, thanks to my prayer and note, we all had a stunning breakthrough in which Janet connected to us on an emotional level and we ended in a big group hug. Or, at least it would be pretty good if I could say that after writing the prayer I reached such a stage of enlightenment that I never got annoyed at Janet again. Neither would be true.

Janet brought my note and prayer to our next meeting. She was excited and pleased that I had sent them to her. She read them out loud to the group, and one of the others said that he had similar feelings about her. Then Janet joyfully plunged into her week's events, in even more arid detail than before. By the time she got to Friday, I was as annoyed as ever. However, along with being annoyed, a new feeling had sneaked into me. What was it? Affection? Compassion? Could this be love? My prayer and note had made Janet feel loved. Thanks to Janet, I had received a great blessing: I had moved to a new place in my spiritual journey. I was grateful to her and wished her well with all my heart. As the weeks passed, that feeling didn't go away.

In getting to know the Episcopalians, I had received a moment of grace, written a prayer that answers itself, and learned something about love. I looked forward to the fall and the return of active church life with the Unitarians. What would I learn from them?

Getting to know the Unitarians

September came around and we Unitarians started up again, now with a quarter-time minister. Rev. Peter Duncan lived in Portland, Oregon. One long weekend each month, he made the four-hour commute to Port Townsend to meet with the fellowship's committees and deliver the sermon at the Sunday service. The other services of the month continued as before, with sermons delivered by a variety of guest speakers. I gladly returned to my rotation between my two churches. Peter's once-a-month preaching provided a spiritual anchor the fellowship needed. On his off-Sundays, the guest speaker could be something of a crap shoot: usually uplifting, inspiring, or at least educational, but sometimes boring, long-winded, or just plain puzzling. And yet I enjoyed even the crap shoot, and the willingness of us Unitarians to take a chance on a new way of looking at things.

While I continued to be drawn to the Episcopal service, especially to the rite of the Eucharist, I also continued to be confounded by Christian doctrine. I struggled with the images of God presented week after week in the Episcopal liturgy. The arbitrary, vengeful Yahweh of the Hebrew Bible repelled me; the loving, nurturing "Father" of the Christian church did not match my observation of the world. Jesus, for all his goodness, remained essentially human in my eyes, and I saw nothing to be gained by turning him into a God after his death. And yet these images of God were given at St. Paul's, to be wrestled with, maybe, but not to be seriously challenged. In contrast, as a Unitarian I met a variety of images of God. Because they weren't presented as articles of faith, I could experience them without the dug-in resistance I felt on my Episcopal weeks.

At one Unitarian Sunday service, our guest speaker was a Unitarian Sikh. He demonstrated to the children how he tied his turban and explained to the adults the history and basic tenets of the Sikh faith. As a congregation, we read responsively from a Sikh morning prayer that included the response, "Not by thought alone can God be known, though one think a hundred thousand times." As an obsessive thinker, I needed to say and hear those words. At the end of the service, our speaker and his wife served each of us a dollop of a sweet, rice-like concoction that's ritually served to the congregation at the end of every Sikh service. That Sunday was surprising, illuminating, and moving.

Another Sunday, we Unitarians recited together a litany adapted by Ralph Waldo Emerson from the Hindu scriptures, *The Bhagavad Gita,* that included the response, "As there is no screen or ceiling between our heads and the infinite heavens, so there is no bar or wall in the soul where we, the effect, cease, and God, the cause, begins." This matched my experiences working in my garden and the woods surrounding our house, especially turning my compost pile, seeing the process of transformation at work, and my feeling that I was intimately a part of it, interchangeable with the orange peels and the millipedes and the rich earth. Later in the responsive reading we read, "Within us is the soul of the whole; the wise silence; the universal beauty, to which every part and particle is equally related; the eternal One. When it breaks through our intellect, it is genius; when it breathes through our will, it is virtue; when it flows through our affections, it is love." Emerson, I learned, had been a staunch Unitarian in his time.

Another Sunday, the children of the fellowship acted out a Buddhist parable. In the parable, a poor woman whose child has died learns that suffering is shared by all human beings, and that only by recognizing the universality of suffering can we give and receive true compassion. Two of the fellowship's children, a girl and a boy, shared the role of the Buddha. The two children sat cross-legged at opposite ends of a long table, alternating the lines of the Buddha between them. By the end of the simple story, I wasn't the only member of the congregation wiping away tears. Part of my emotion came from the feeling of shared human suffering that the parable was designed to evoke. Another part came from seeing God as a boy-child and a girl-child sharing their words of wisdom with us adults. It was as powerful and moving an image of God as I saw in church that year.

During the announcements one Unitarian Sunday, a member of the congregation I knew only by sight stood and announced that she had ordered the course materials for "Building Your Own Theology," a class developed and refined in Unitarian church workshops and now available from the national Unitarian Universalist Association. The purpose of the class, she said, was to lead participants through the process of developing a personal credo, or statement of belief. She and two other women planned to offer the course to the fellowship in the spring, acting as co-facilitators and rotating responsibility for the sessions. The class would meet once a week after church on Sundays for eight weeks. Bring your own sack lunch and end up with your own personal statement of belief. Sign up in the back of the hall after the service.

My initial reaction to the idea of an eight-week class for building my own theology was that we Unitarians certainly had our nerve. Give or take a few centuries, it had taken Judeo-Christian theology five thousand years to reach its current state. And we Unitarians thought we could each build our own in *eight weeks*? How could the class offer any more than a superficial quick-fix for spiritual emptiness?

While one part of my mind boggled at Unitarian hubris, a different part asked, "Well, Margaret, if this class is too superficial for you, then what do you mean when you say 'Dear God'? You haven't exactly cozied up to the Trinity, so what is it? Aren't you trying to build your own theology right now? How's it going?"

When the lay leader blew out the chalice candle at the end of the service, and while the congregation surged toward the coffee and cookies, I marched to the back of the room and signed up to build my own theology. In the weeks before the course started, twelve other Unitarians signed up, too.

The class met in the library of the community center where we held our church services. The small, book-lined room was mostly taken up by three library tables shoved together to form a U. At the first meeting, I looked around the tables at my fellow theologians. Most were older than me; our oldest class member was a man in his eighties. Across from me sat a woman artist who worked with fabric; she wore one of her pieces, a gorgeous vest of multi-colored woven threads. Our facilitator was a writer like me. She lighted a candle in a chalice and passed out a syllabus. Then she asked us to go around the table, introduce ourselves, say something about our religious background, and explain why we were there. It was just like the initial meeting of my spiritual discussion group at St. Paul's.

At first, it seemed to me we Unitarians were very different from us Episcopalians. In my St. Paul's group, all but one of us had grown up in the Christian church, and most were life-long Episcopalians. In contrast, the thirteen fledgling theologians around the table that Sunday included only two who had grown up in the Unitarian church. The rest of us were either refugees from one Christian denomination or another or had grown up with no religious observances at all. One of the two life-long Unitarians in the class said this mix was typical of Unitarian congregations.

What we had in common was not a single religious background, but a pile of education and skepticism. Each member of the group had attended college, and we held a fair number of advanced degrees among us. Except for me, no one was interested in defining God. Some doubted whether the final assignment of the course was worth doing at all. They'd left Christian churches specifically to get away from creeds and statements of belief, and so why should they write one now, even a personal one? One of the men said firmly that he expected to produce a statement of his highest values, with no "belief" attached to it in any way, shape, or form. Our facilitator assured him that was just fine. Whatever he wanted.

No other member of the group shared my exact goals for the class; still, as I listened to each, I heard echoes and reflections of my own search for meaning. George, a recovering alcoholic and artist who worked at a local candle factory, spoke of a growing conviction that "faith" didn't have to mean belief in a supernatural force, but could mean faith in himself and the people he loved. If he could achieve that kind of faith, he would be happy. Wanda, a nurse, spoke of how her work drained not only her energy but also her spirit, and that she needed to re-connect with whatever gave her the energy and compassion to face another day. Henry, a retired systems analyst who had been raised in the Episcopal church, explained that he had rejected religion in his youth, raising science and math in its place. Today, however, he found more satisfaction in walking through a forest than in writing algorithms. "I hugged a tree and got something back," he said. "What was it? It was a mystery. There is no place for belief in my life, but I want to find a place for that mystery."

Exactly. Like Henry and others around the room, I was there because I wanted to get closer to the mystery, but only if I could do it without abandoning what I perceived to be true in the world.

By the time the last person at the table spoke, I was ready to go along with this crowd wherever they wanted to go. My skepticism about whether we could build a theology in eight weeks had melted away; obviously nobody at the table thought we'd really do that, anyway. Instead, I felt a kind of shared hope, or confidence, that by putting our minds to it we could come up with something meaningful. We required no ordained persons to help us with this work, thank you very much, and no professors of theology. We had a course outline and willing facilitators—not teachers, they emphasized—and we would take it from there. I left the class happy, clutching my first assignment and ready to get to work.

At home that night, I sat at my desk and read over the assignment. We were to write a spiritual autobiography. The assignment included an outline that listed what I was supposed to include in the autobiography. I could see from the outline that it wouldn't be short. I was supposed to include descriptions of places where significant things happened to me, accounts of people who'd had an impact on my life, two or three formative experiences, communities that had a lasting influence on my development, two or three of the most important life decisions I'd made, religious or spiritual experiences I'd had, the happiest and saddest experiences of my life, and theological values that had informed me. Whoever developed this course was going to make me work for it.

To start, the instructions said to draw a horizontal line on a page, put the year of my birth at the start of the line and a reasonable expectation of the year of my death at the end. Mark where the current year would be, to show where I was now in the chronology of my life, then write how I felt about being there.

I took out a clean sheet of paper, drew a line, put 1951 on the left end, and then asked myself how old I expected to be when I died. Seventy-five, the average life expectancy of a newborn girl? That didn't seem quite right. Both my mother's mother and my father's mother had lived past their 91st birthdays. A great-grandmother on my mother's side also lived to 91. A great-grandmother on my father's side lived to 77. She was chopping wood, missed her target and struck her leg with the ax, then treated herself at home until blood poisoning killed her. My own mother was still alive and healthy in her 70s.

My mother's good health, the evidence of three female ancestors who lived to their 90s and the reasonable conviction that a woman who chops her own wood at 77 could have lived to 90 with luck and careful aim, made me think I wasn't crazy to expect to reach 90 myself. I did the math, made the mark, and discovered that if my projection were accurate, I was exactly halfway through my life.

Born 1951　　　　　　　1996　　　　　　　Die 2041

45 years old

How did I feel about that? After the initial shock of having my mortality jump off the page at me, I didn't feel too bad. The first half of my life hadn't been totally wasted. I loved my husband, David, felt loved by him, and was on speaking terms with everyone in my family. I had friends. I'd written some stuff I thought was good.

There were plenty of things I still wanted to do. If I died that night, I'd think my promise didn't come to full bloom. On the other hand, if I lived to 90 and had good health, I might just have enough time.

After writing down those feelings, I closed my notebook, satisfied that I'd done enough for the first day. I felt grounded by my timeline and what it meant to be in the middle of my life. I knew where I stood and had the sensation of starting on a new adventure.

As it happened, our "Building Your Own Theology" class started the same week as Lent. We Unitarians don't take much notice of Lent. In fact, I doubt if more than two or three Unitarians in the fellowship were aware of it at all. By contrast, Lent was big news at St. Paul's. We Episcopalians require a good deal of repentance in our liturgy, and Lent gives us everything along those lines we could hope for. St. Paul's had a tradition of Wednesday night soup-and-prayer-ful-discussion meetings during Lent, and I decided to go to them that year. As a result, during the five weeks of Lent I got a dose of Unitarian theology-discussion Sunday afternoons, followed by a dose of Episcopal Lenten-discussion Wednesday evenings. In each group, we described spiritual or religious events in our lives and tried to find meaning in those events. As I spoke and listened, those first-impression differences I'd seen between the Episcopalians and the Unitarians began to look thin and superficial, while what we had in common revealed its depth.

In the Lenten discussion group at St. Paul's, an Episcopal woman who runs a family farm with her husband described walking alone in the woods near her home, telling her concerns to God, and receiving back not necessarily an answer, but peace and strength for the day. A photographer told of visiting a dying friend in the hospital and having the powerful vision of his friend's body in the arms of God. A weaver told of sitting alone in her bedroom, lighting a candle, and praying from an ancient liturgy.

In the "Building Your Own Theology" group at Quimper, a Unitarian musician described walking in an ancient forest with his wife and feeling connection, peace. A nurse talked about her encounters with death in her work and its effect on the lives of the people who stayed behind. A retired botany professor told of singing in Mahler's Eighth Symphony with a huge, multi-chorus concert, an entire soprano section that finished the piece in tears, a standing ovation that went on and on.

I told both groups about witnessing the births of each of my four nephews and how that made me feel about being human and part of a human family. The two groups used different words to react to my story—God and spirit; life, hope, and joy—but I felt the commonality under the words more than the differences on the surface. In both groups, we were trying to do a similar thing: find meaning and connection within ourselves and beyond ourselves.

At the end of the "Building Your Own Theology" class, we each wrote our personal credo, put them together in a little booklet, and printed one out for every member of the group. My credo was one of the few statements of belief from the class that mentioned God by name. With much backpedaling and expressions of uncertainty, in my credo I tried to tell what I thought I was doing when I prayed. At the end, I included the prayer that I wrote for Janet in my Episcopal discussion group, the prayer to the God who made the rocks just the way they are, rising from the earth.

It took that Unitarian theology workshop for me to find the space and support I needed to come to terms with the God I prayed to in the Episcopal church. Most of the Episcopalians I know are theologically tolerant, and the Episcopalians at St. Paul's didn't seem to mind having a member with problems with Christian theology. Nobody ever tried to twist my arm about it. At the same time, the theology the Episcopal church had all "ready to go," from the Nicene Creed near the beginning of the *Book of Common Prayer* to the catechism near its end, did little to help me find my God. The Nicene Creed was a bit too much for my stage of theology, and I found the catechism oppressive rather than informative. I didn't like having both the questions and the answers handed to me at the same time.

And yet, to my surprise, by the time I wrote my credo at the end of the Unitarian workshop, I was finally able to say parts of the Nicene Creed and mean what I said.

Lent and Holy Week both had passed before the "Building Your Own Theology" class ended, so the Wednesday night soup meetings had also ended. In the Lent group we had learned the *Lectio Divina*, a centuries-old method of meditation through scripture, and it was now a part of my daily morning routine. As the weeks of spring turning into summer came and went, I thought back on the two groups and what I got from each: good talk, good soup, some insight, a piece of homemade apricot breakfast bread, respectful attention and support, a bit of love given and received, a small step closer to God. I was struck by how different they were, and how much the same, and how I wouldn't want to give up one for the other.

To go where I wanted to go, I needed both. In the Episcopalians and the Unitarians, I had finally found my team.

Chapter VI

Liturgy, History, and Ritual

Getting to know the Episcopalians and the Unitarians, sharing beliefs and struggles about beliefs, trying to care for each other—that side of church life had sneaked up on me and moved me along my spiritual path in an unexpected way. In the meantime, the rhythm of Sunday services, first one and then the other, deepened my attachment to each church.

"Liturgy" is what we church people *do* for an hour or so on a Sunday morning. It includes all the words, the music, the standing, sitting, kneeling, listening, and praying. Like my first impression of the Episcopalians and Unitarians themselves, the liturgies of my two churches at first seemed to have little in common.

Juggling the prayer book

In my Methodist upbringing, to follow a Sunday service all I needed was the week's order of service handed out at the door and a hymnal. By the time I quit church in my late teens, I was an old hand, standing and sitting with hardly a glance at the asterisked cues in the order of service, singing the doxology as if it were hard-wired between my brain and voice box, and using the order of service as a place mark for the next hymn, just like my Dad did.

At St. Paul's, I was bumped right off that raft of complacency and into a sea of confusion. St. Paul's was a prayer-book parish, which means that services followed the order and wording laid out in the Episcopal *Book of Common Prayer*. At my initial Episcopal service I didn't quite grasp the principle of the thing at first and was startled when everyone around me said words in unison that they knew and I didn't. I studied the order of service and saw that not only the hymns, but also other elements of the service had page numbers attached to them. These numbers referred to pages in the red *Book of Common Prayer* available in the pew racks next to the purple hymnal. My first few weeks as an Episcopalian, I spent a good deal of the services juggling the prayer book, the hymnal, and the week's order of service, always one step behind everybody else. It didn't help that St. Paul's holds two services each Sunday, one at eight o'clock (using Rite I, traditional language) and another at ten o'clock (using Rite II, modern language). Rite I and Rite II start on different pages in the prayer book. To avoid separate printings, St. Paul's included both orders of service in its weekly bulletin, printed on facing pages. At any given moment during the service, I could be looking in the hymnal for a response that appears only in the prayer book, in the prayer book for a hymn, or on the wrong page of the prayer book because I had inadvertently looked up the page for the eight o'clock service instead of the ten o'clock. By the time I figured out where we were, everybody else had closed whatever book I was holding and picked up the other one.

On my second Sunday at St. Paul's, during the moment in the service when we Episcopalians wish each other the peace of the Lord, an older woman in the pew behind me shook my hand, said, "The peace of the Lord be always with you," then smiled into my eyes, gave my hand an extra squeeze and whispered, "Don't worry, dear, you'll get used to it."

She was right. Gradually, I got used to it. After I grasped the basic structure of the service, it dawned on me that a good portion of the words I heard and spoke each week were exactly the same as last week. I learned the shorter responses by heart so as not to have to flip through the prayer book to find them. But I had to stay on my toes;

the Episcopal liturgy didn't let me zone out completely. My first weeks at St. Paul's passed during Lent, when the Episcopal service is at its most penitential. After Lent ended at Easter, we stopped saying the confession and started adding *alleluias* to our responses. Seven weeks later, at Pentecost, the confession came back, but the *alleluias* stayed. And yet within these changes the basic, underlying text of the service held steady and gradually became familiar to me. We did it the same way, again and again, with purposeful variations.

A good story is worth repeating. After so many tellings, its words become like the surface of a clear stream, and you look through them to see the tadpoles, shiners, water moss, bug larvae, crawdaddies, stones, and clay that make up the whole. Religious language can be mind-bogglingly metaphoric (*you're washed white as snow in the blood of the Lamb*), or so abstract it creates the sensation of stepping into empty air (*we will find eternal peace*). When you stand on the outside and look in, the language of religion sometimes seems either to be full of lies or to mean nothing at all. But when you step across the threshold and stand inside, then the religion's language miraculously stretches to take you in.

Doctrine was a problem for me at St. Paul's, and yet it had its function: doctrine gave me something to fight against. It was a context against which I could form my own ideas. I knew when I attended my first Episcopal service that I would never mouth the words of the Nicene Creed just to fit in, and we Episcopalians, God help us, say the Creed at every service. So in my Episcopal church, I was forced to ask what, exactly, I held sacred, and whether I admitted any power greater than myself. The surprising thing was how often the answers could live in the many layers of the language of the liturgy ... once I let go of the sticky surface and started to dive.

But before diving, I needed information about what I was diving into. I'd read the Nicene Creed in my Methodist youth, but if I ever knew where it came from or what it was meant to do, by now I had forgotten. So I got some references and did some reading about it, hoping I'd find out why we Episcopalians were so attached to the thing.

Grappling with the Creed

The Nicene Creed is named after a city in Asia Minor. In the fourth century after Jesus' birth, Constantine called the top dogs of the Christian church together in the town of Nicaea to clarify the tenets of the Christian faith. Back then (as now) Christians believed all kinds of things. Some believed that Jesus was so completely divine, he couldn't have been really human or born of a woman, but must have descended directly to earth in a blaze of glory. Others believed that Jesus was entirely human. He might have been the best human being ever, but he was still only human, made by God just like us.

In Nicaea, the dominant Christian clergy laid down the law in the Nicene Creed: Jesus Christ was both thoroughly human and thoroughly God. He was born of a human woman and died a human death. He was also *"light from light, true God from true God."* He was not made by God, like we were. Rather, he was begotten by God, an important distinction in the Fourth Century theological wars. If you believed that he either wasn't human or wasn't divine, you believed heresy.

The Nicene Creed was written to be inclusive. Together, Christians could say *"We believe . . . ,"* and declare both who they were and that they were all part of this big spiritual event—the birth, death, and resurrection of Jesus Christ.

It was also written to be exclusive. The established church used the Nicene Creed to determine who was a real Christian and who wasn't. So Christianity took a fateful step toward orthodoxy.

That was the sticky surface, and I found it sticky indeed, being of the personal opinion that Jesus of Nazareth was most likely human in precisely the same way I was human. My Episcopal church didn't use the Nicene Creed to exclude the chaff from the wheat. Nobody seemed to notice or care if I said it on any given Sunday, and I was welcome to take communion regardless. And yet even in its inclusive sense, the Nicene Creed gave me trouble. Was I really part of this crowd? Did I really believe what they believed?

After months of reading, talking, and thinking—and after eight weeks of building my own theology with the Unitarians—I finally got to the point where I could say almost all the Nicene Creed without a blush. What did the trick was asking myself a different question. Instead of asking "Do I believe what they believe?"—which was unanswerable, since I can't read minds other than my own—I began to ask "Can these words be receptacles for what I do believe?" I found the answer was often, "Yes."

But it was a lot of work. During the whole recitation of the Creed, I'd have this subtext going in my brain: "... *okay, Margaret, now when you say 'Father,' you're talking about the creative force in the universe. Could be the laws of physics and chaos, that's fine, but it's the creative force. Okay, now when you say 'Son,' you're talking about an act of transformation that unites you with creation, so when you feel separated, you can be whole again. Can be as simple as a walk in the woods or as hard as finding forgiveness for a major screw-up, but we're basically talking about change and reconciliation here. Okay, now when you say 'Virgin' ...*."

Achieving my personal translation of the Nicene Creed was a good exercise, and I didn't think my translation wreaked too much violence on the underlying meaning of the words. Still, I never liked saying the Creed. A good metaphor works by bringing life and depth to its underlying meaning. The father-son metaphor achieved that life and depth for many Christians over many centuries. However, to me, much of the metaphoric language in the Creed shrank and constricted God. Intellectually, I could see what the metaphors were getting at, but I had to work for them. A living metaphor reaches out and grabs you; it doesn't require you to chip away the strata of centuries to find its meaning.

In addition, I never got over my problems with both the inclusiveness and the exclusiveness of the Creed. When I stand up with a group of people and say *"We believe* . . . ,*"* then I need to know what it is I'm saying, and if I'm not saying what anybody else in the room is saying, then I'd just as soon keep my mouth shut. Which is what I did when we got to the Creed on most of my Episcopal Sundays.

So there I was at St. Paul's, twice a month, choking on the Nicene Creed, and then slipping into the second half of the liturgy like a hot child into a cool lake: praying the prayers of the people, facing my shortcomings, asking for forgiveness, opening my heart to be reconciled to whatever it is we humans hold sacred, and then doing it in the simplest, most direct way I could imagine, by eating and drinking food made holy by the people who joined me in this act of faith.

The real presence

I had no problem with the part of the service called the Eucharist, more commonly known as communion. No problem with the idea that at the communion table I encountered the "real presence" of God. In fact, after struggling with symbol and metaphor through much of the liturgy, it was a tremendous relief to finally set them aside and meet up with the real thing.

In my Protestant youth, I'd heard the unsettling story that Roman Catholics believed the priest actually changed their communion wafers and wine into real flesh and blood, the body and blood of Jesus Christ, and therefore, God. Then the Catholics had to eat and drink Jesus, or they went to hell. We Protestants were not so priest-dominated. The torn-up pieces of WonderBread and little shot glasses of grape juice we shared at communion were *symbols* of the body and blood of Jesus Christ. In eating and drinking them together, we enacted our communion with Him, with each other, and with all Christians. But they were not Jesus' real flesh and blood; they were not really God; and our minister was powerless to change them. They were just symbols.

It was years before I realized that what I'd been told about the Roman Catholic mass was Protestant propaganda, a twisted and exaggerated rendering of the doctrine of transubstantiation. I can't speak for the Pope, or for any other practicing Catholic, but I doubt if many of them think they're drinking fresh blood and eating raw flesh during the Eucharist. I can't speak for the people who sat around me in the pews when I was a child, either. I don't know what they thought they were doing when they drank that grape juice. Personally, I thought I was drinking grape juice, and I liked it very much. I can only try to say what happened for me during the Eucharist at St. Paul's.

The language of the Eucharist makes the wafer and wine into symbols of body and blood—the body and blood of God on earth. When I participated in the Eucharist at St. Paul's, however, I did not act out a pretend encounter between me and a symbolic God: I encountered the real thing. I may not have known what I meant by God, but I knew that whatever I prayed to was present in every atom of the universe. The way I saw it, the rite of the Eucharist was designed not to symbolically create that presence, which was there anyway, but to use symbols to *make me aware of it* in a particular way. If I were truly and completely enlightened, I wouldn't require the sacraments of the church to make me aware of the real presence of God; every second of my life would be sacramental. But I wasn't truly and completely enlightened. And so in the Eucharist, I was made aware of the presence of God by the intimate and erotic act of eating and drinking bread and wine we had ritually named the body and blood of God's incarnation on earth. When the wafer touched my tongue and the wine touched my lips, God was present. Really. The purpose of everything happening around me was to open me up, so that I could encounter the real presence of God.

On most Sundays, it worked.

Heretics and cliff-jumpers

It was different with us Unitarians. We had no thorny creeds or blood-drinking rituals. We had those seven principles, but otherwise, you could believe anything you pleased. You could be a Unitarian atheist, agnostic, secular humanist, Christian or refugee from Christianity, worshipper of the Great Goddess, student of Buddhism, Taoism, or the spirituality of the First Nations. You could be any combination of the above. You name it, we had it. We could no more have stood up all together and said *"We believe . . . "* than we could have swallowed burgundy and called it God.

At earlier points in our history, we Unitarians did have some doctrine; that's how we got our name. The first Unitarians were those very people, back in the Fourth Century, who thought that Jesus was wholly human. They split from the established church over the Trinity, saying that God was a Unity, not a Father, Son and Spirit combo. The Nicene Creed relegated Unitarians to a heretical branch of Christianity where they remained for centuries. During the heyday of the Inquisition, Unitarians were burned at the stake for their theology.

The Universalists, on the other hand, split from the established church over the question of who gets saved. Universalists believed that God's grace would ultimately save everybody, so there was no hell. This viewpoint wasn't quite as threatening to orthodoxy as Unitarianism. I don't know of any Universalists who burned at the stake for not believing in hell. However, they lost the doctrine wars, too, and endured their own persecutions.

Despite marginal status, both the Unitarians and the Universalists hung on through the centuries, gradually calling into question more and more aspects of orthodox Christian religion. Over time, both groups developed a remarkable practice: instead of replacing doctrine they didn't like with new doctrine, they changed its status to opinion and agreed to disagree. In contrast to the traditional church, which built up its doctrine brick by brick, doctrine gradually melted away. Both groups became havens for prominent intellectuals and champions of social justice. In 1961 the two churches in America merged into the Unitarian Universalist Association, and the new denomination was a hotbed of rationality, a comfortable home for atheists, agnostics, and humanists who held that human values and the power of the human spirit and intellect were enough—more than enough—to carry the human race through its time on earth.

When I first started attending the Quimper Fellowship, the U.U. "faith" seemed like a vacuum to me. The seven principles of the Unitarian Universalist Association were just principles; where was the *faith*? And yet Unitarians often referred to their "faith" as being different from faiths based on doctrine, but a faith nonetheless. It took awhile for me to see that the fourth U.U. principle, "*A free and responsible search for truth and meaning*," could be a matter of faith. We Unitarians were like scientists, putting our faith in the search for truth, not in any particular truth. We were like artists, putting our faith in the process of creating art, not in any individual finished piece. It was a little like stepping off a cliff into empty air. You aren't alone on the cliff; in fact, you're surrounded by cliff-jumpers. The tools are there, and the support of the other people in the church is there. But both the question and the answer, both the medium and the finished work of art, are entirely up to you. In stark contrast to the Episcopal church's outpouring of doctrine and scripture, we Unitarians provided our own context.

In the back of the Unitarian hymnal, you'll find about a hundred pages of suggested readings for lay leaders to use during the service. (Just suggestions. Perfectly okay to bring your own.) Those pages include poetry, aphorisms, prayers, scriptures, and responsive readings, some written by contemporary writers such as Annie Dillard, Wendell Berry, or Starhawk; others by ancient writers such as the author of Ecclesiastes or *The Bhagavad Gita*; pieces by writers of different races, many faiths, diverse cultures. This goes along with the Unitarian notion that truth is revealed in many ways throughout the world. That, in fact, we all have truth inside us, and it's our job to dig it out.

In contrast, lay readers at St. Paul's had no choice over the week's readings. We followed the lectionary, a three-year cycle of Bible readings all laid out for us near the end of the prayer book. If I attended Episcopal services for the rest of my life, eventually I would hear the same sets of readings many times, once every three years, besides hearing the same words and sentences in other parts of the liturgy every week.

I liked the repetition in the liturgy at St. Paul's; it helped me find myself in the layers of meaning. But repetition has its weaknesses as well as its strengths. Repetition can reveal layers of meaning; it can also suck out any meaning and leave a dry husk behind. You can get so attached to the specific words of the liturgy, you come to feel that it's those exact words, and not the layers underneath, that matter. Then if the words change, you have a problem. I knew that some of my Episcopal friends were still shuddering from the earthquake that hit their faith when the church updated the language in the prayer book back in the 1970s.

We Unitarians, we didn't have repetitive language in our service. The general form of our service was fairly standard, but the words were never the same. And just as I liked the repetition at St.

Paul's, I liked the variety at the Quimper Fellowship. It's true that repetition peels back layers of meaning, but variation can show new angles, new perspectives, a different side of the same mystery. For a while, I thought that potlucks were the only rituals we Unitarians had, but I was wrong. We didn't do it every week like the Episcopalians, but it turned out that we did have a ritual for communion, as I discovered one Sunday morning in May. My first Unitarian Flower Communion expanded my view of holy communion in a way that repetition alone could not achieve.

A daisy and a sage blossom

It was a typical Pacific Northwest spring day, cool, breezy, the sky mostly gray with spots of blue. Throughout the drive to the community center, I enjoyed the dandelions in full force along the side of the county road and the native pink rhododendron just starting to burst out. When I arrived, I was greeted at the door by a teenager holding a basket of flowers. "Did you bring a flower?" she asked. When I said no, she offered the basket. "Then take one. Everybody needs a flower for the service."

I noticed that the other people walking up to the door all carried flowers. A woman holding a spray of flame-colored gladiolas edged past me into the meeting room, followed by a man holding two wilted dandelions. This was one of the flaws of being an every-other-week church member; I missed announcements half the time in both my churches and often didn't know what was going on. I was embarrassed to be flowerless on this day when everybody else knew to bring flowers, and I quickly picked a scrawny white daisy out of the basket and took a seat.

During the first part of the service, I held my daisy and looked around at the other flowers in the room. Plenty of pink native rhodies.

Early roses, red clover, wild mustard. The air tasted sweet. Since I'm allergic to a wide range of pollens, I found myself digging for a handkerchief.

After the opening announcements, the lay leader told us it was Flower Communion Sunday, which was why everybody had a flower. She said that Unitarian Universalist congregations around the world celebrate this communion in the spring, though not all on the same Sunday, and not exactly the same way, since most congregations develop their own variation on the theme.

She asked the children in the congregation to come to the front, gave each one an empty basket, and told them to pass among us all, gathering in the flowers. When a kid got to my row, my daisy took its place among the clover and rhodies and wild mustard. After they'd gathered all the flowers, the children deposited their baskets on a table in the front of the room.

Then the lay leader spoke a few words about sharing and community. How the word "sharing" contains in its meaning both giving and receiving; how a "community" is a group of people in which each member gives, and each receives. When she finished, the children took up the baskets and passed among us again, and this time we each picked out a flower to take away with us.

How can I say what happened to those flowers between the time the children gathered them in and the time I picked out one to take home? That's the thing about ritual: we use objects—flowers, candles, bread, grape juice, wine—to be the physical presence of something that we can hardly say.

Even though I hadn't known to bring a flower, by the time I dropped my daisy in the basket I was willing to think it was mine. When the basket came around again for me to pick out a flower to take home, all the flowers from all the people were mixed together so I couldn't tell who brought what anyway. Each flower was its own self, perfect even in its bruises and flaws. Each flower was necessary to make up the whole bouquet; each was its own gift.

I had made the mental move from flower to human before I knew I was moving. I picked out a sprig of sage blossoms, unassuming, raggedy little blue flowers with dust-dull leaves, but so fragrant! I sniffed them during the rest of the service, carried them home with me, and put them on my desk. Each day that week their fragrance reminded me that it was through my life that I made my gift, and that just being alive meant that I deserved the gift of life.

That's why I went to church. I didn't go to church to be good, even though my churches provided opportunities to be good if I wanted to be: soup kitchens, care for the sick, stuff like that. I didn't go because I was bad and needed forgiveness, though my churches did provide the opportunity to work out some redemption when I needed it. I went to church because I was human, I was trying to figure out what that meant and how to do it, and as far as I could tell that's what the Episcopalians and the Unitarians were doing.

Chapter VII

Dear God

I had started to pray, didn't know what I was praying to, and had to know. On one level, praying helped me with some issues in my life. On another level, it made me feel silly. Though I had a variety of reasons for returning to church after a twenty-five-year absence, mostly I came back to figure out who, or what, received my prayers.

Between the time I started to pray and the time I returned to church, I talked about this problem to a few people, some church-going, some not. A man who didn't go to church suggested that I was simply using the form of prayer to talk to myself. He didn't see any problem with that. If it helped me to talk to myself as "Dear God," he thought that was fine. I saw the truth of what he was saying (after getting over the feeling of being patronized), and yet it wasn't good enough. I often talk to myself; I like talking to myself. My prayers felt different from those conversations. In prayer, I was trying to get a perspective on the situation other than my own. A perspective greater than my own. My prayers were directed both inward and outward. To what? I had to know.

A woman who did go to church suggested that you never know exactly what you're praying to anyway, so it wasn't worth fussing about. You prayed, and God was always a mystery. That was where faith came in. You just had faith that God was out there hearing your prayers. I felt the truth of what she was saying, too, and yet it wasn't good enough either. This was before I started to build my own theology with the Unitarians or encounter God in the Episcopal Eucharist, and God was a complete blank to me. How can you have faith in a complete blank? I had to have *some* idea.

It might have been easier to come to an idea of God if I'd had no religious background at all, because the road that led to a blank God began at the doorways of my Sunday School classrooms.

From mighty love to nothing at all

As a kid, I received lots of information about God. A book of Bible stories for children was in our bookshelves at home, and I read it for pleasure more than once. Every week I heard a Bible story in Sunday School, then colored in pictures from the story. In fact, my sharpest recollections of the religion I got as a child are images—pictures I colored, pictures from story books, pictures in Bibles.

I still have in my mind's eye the picture of a shaft of light striking down between waves and land, and beneath it these words printed: "God said, Let the waters under the heaven be gathered together unto one place, and let the dry land appear." I crayoned the shaft of light yellow, the land brown, and the waves blue. I remember the image of Joshua with his priests blowing their trumpets outside the stone walls of Jericho, and the stones beginning to fall. Daniel in the den of lions, uneaten. The baby Jesus in the manger, surrounded by cows and sheep. The grownup Jesus surrounded by children, other grownups off to one side. Jesus glowing on a mountain top, three disciples kneeling beside him.

I don't have childhood images of the crucifixion, other than small crucifixes hanging on church walls. I don't think I ever colored in a crucifixion. Maybe they skipped that scene in the coloring books. But I do remember a picture of the ascension, Christ rising straight up into heaven, his face full of love, his arms outstretched.

From these images, and from the stories and teachings that

came with them, I thought I knew what God was. God was in charge. God created everything and watched over everything. God was all-powerful, and God loved me—me personally—along with every other human being who ever lived. If I had drawn a picture of God then, I might have drawn a big heart with muscular cartoon arms coming out the sides. Mighty love.

---

illus to be added

However, when I prayed in my childhood, I didn't pray to a heart with muscular arms. I prayed to a bearded old white man in the sky, just like everybody else I knew. The stories of God's omnipotence and the power of faith went straight to my hopeful young soul. I distinctly remember the Sunday School lesson when Jesus chastised the disciples for their lack of faith. I was about nine years old. Jesus told the disciples that if their faith were strong enough, they could do anything. He said they could throw a mountain into the sea if they had enough faith, and that whatever they prayed for in faith, they would receive. I was ready to believe it, and also to believe that my faith was stronger than the faith of those witless disciples. I would show Jesus what faith could be.

My Sunday School teacher warned us about this particular passage. She sat at the head of the table where we colored pictures and explained that faith powerful enough to move mountains is extremely unusual in human beings. She also explained that you have to ask for the right sort of thing. Jesus was talking about a particular kind of faith, and it wasn't the kind that provides chocolate bars for little boys and girls, just for the asking. If you asked with the right kind of faith, then you'd automatically ask for the right kind of thing.

I didn't give much weight to my Sunday School teacher's opinions about faith. She was putting her own slant on Jesus' words. Jesus didn't say you had to ask for the right kind of thing. His example involved throwing a mountain into the sea. Was that "the right kind of thing"? He also said, straight out, no back-pedaling or wishy-washy language, that if you had the faith, you'd get what you asked for. So I went with Jesus' words rather than my Sunday School teacher's.

One night in early December, I lay in bed and asked God for a dog for Christmas. I told God I knew he could get me a dog and had faith that he would. I felt the warm furry body next to mine, the cold nose on my neck.

> Jesus answered them, "Truly I tell you, if you have faith and do not doubt, . . . even if you say to this mountain, 'Be lifted up and thrown into the sea,' it will be done. Whatever you ask for in prayer with faith, you will receive."
>
> —Matthew 21:21-22 (New Revised Standard Version)

I worked myself into a trance of rock-hard conviction that it was a done deal. If faith could truly move mountains, I would have my dog.

It turned out my parents' faith that we would not get a dog, without any effort on their part that I could see, was more powerful than mine.

Does every Christian child experience the same loss of faith over those Bible verses? That Christmas night, after all the presents were opened and thoroughly possessed, I went to bed and said my prayers in a new way. It's hard to be angry and cynical on Christmas night. My family wasn't rich, but my parents knew their children and I always received at least one Christmas present that thrilled me

completely. One Christmas it was colored plastic beads that fit together to make jewelry. Another, a pink diary with its own lock and
key. I don't remember the particular gift that won me over that
Christmas, but I do remember that I couldn't be angry while in thrall
of this new possession.

Still, when it came to saying prayers, things were different between me and God. I held back. I asked God to bless Mom and Dad
and Rose and Brian, like I always did. Presumably, God would do
that. But I didn't ask for anything I wanted. I had my pride, if not my
puppy. Weeks passed before I broke down and started to ask God for
things again. It was so hard not to! But even then, I always asked with
a certain cool distance.

"If You feel like it, such-and-so would be nice."

"Here's what I want, in case You're interested."

I didn't expect much in return, and I don't remember that God
ever came through for me in the way I asked.

At some point I got the information from Sunday School that
God wasn't really an old man in the sky. God was much greater than
that and existed everywhere all the time. I still heard from all the au-
thorities that God loved me, but I wasn't so sure about that love anymore. Compared to the immediacy of my parent's love, God's seemed
kind of theoretical. At least my parents said straight out that we
couldn't have a dog. They didn't tell me that I could have one if I
wished hard enough, except I could never wish hard enough.

However, I still thought of God as the all-powerful and intelligent being who created the world. Some of my high school classmates
were shedding their religious beliefs like butterflies emerging from
cocoons, but I had a defense of God all ready for them. In any discussion on the existence of God, I would point dramatically out a window
and ask, "Do you see that tree?" Yes, they did. Then I told them tri-
umphantly, "That tree proves God exists."

I'd learned enough in high school biology to know that a tree was a fine piece of craftsmanship, finer than anything we humans had ever come up with. God was the intelligence that designed the tree and all the rest of the universe. If I'd drawn an image of God then, I might have drawn a tree with light bulbs and zigzag lines showing the brains and power that made it.

illustration to be added

Mine was a brittle kind of faith, easily snapped. As high school classes matured into college courses, I stopped going to church. It wasn't long before Botany 101 made it clear that, given enough time, random evolution, using no discernible intelligence at all, could produce a tree. Geology 101 proved that evolution had had plenty of time for trees and even for human beings. A single lecture in Philosophy 101 demonstrated that the existence of God could neither be logically proved nor disproved. In a few months, it was all over. My picture of God had transformed into nothing at all.

Casting about for God's Image

illustration to be added

Twenty years passed before I prayed again. When I did start praying for help, I didn't know what I was praying to, except that it wasn't a muscular heart, an old man, or a lightning bolt with brains. I prayed to a mystery.

Sometimes I was simply aware of the mystery. I saw a flash of it during a trip to New York that David and I took before we were married. We were walking on a busy sidewalk in Manhattan. I don't remember if it was day or night. A man with a wound on his forehead came toward us. His damp, ragged hair might have been clotted with blood, or maybe it was only dirt. He wore deeply dirty clothes. His red, swollen hands, cupped in half-fists, swung loosely at his sides. His eyes were focused somewhere past my right shoulder. He staggered while he walked. The sidewalk traffic flowed around him and with him. He was strange and frightening, and at the same time he belonged on the Manhattan sidewalk as much as any of us. It was that paradox—that he could be both alien and resident, both brutalized and human, that he could stand out in the moving mass of people like a sea monster in a school of tuna and at the same time be as much at home as any of us—that stayed with me. I never saw him again, but I remember him often, and when I do, I am aware of the mystery.

Years later, I was out on our property on the Olympic Peninsula, cutting a path through the woods. This was before our house was built. After chopping through dense salal and hacking off ironwood bushes for an hour or so, I stopped, exhausted. I found myself standing motionless, intensely aware of all the life around me, the breathing moss, the chattering birds, the living earth. I was as much a part of the woods as any millipede or cedar tree. At that moment, too, I was aware of the mystery.

Sometimes I wanted to speak to this mystery directly. Out of habit, I began with Dear God and ended with Amen. But I thought to myself, "I'm not praying to that old man in the sky. Rather, I'm praying to this thing I can't define." It was sort of like talking into a foggy valley.

Praying into a fog bank requires a lot of effort. I wanted an image to focus on when I prayed. I wanted something to pray *to*. But I couldn't go back to that old man; he was too closely associated with all I'd left behind.

At first I wondered if the problem was the male image of God. Maybe it would help to change genders. This was still before I had returned to any traditional church. If God was the creator, then how about an image of a God capable of giving birth?

So I tried saying "Dear Goddess" at the beginning of my prayers instead of "Dear God." But Dear Goddess made me feel even sillier than Dear God did. The word "Goddess," like the word "Negress," conveys variation rather than essence. There is the thing itself (God), and then there is the female version of the thing itself (Goddess). I wasn't praying to a version, but to the thing itself. Besides, using "Goddess" to address a female image of God boxed the word "God" even further into the male image, which was not the direction I wanted to go.

So I decided to change my name for God. The name "Via" suggested a way or path; it contained an echo of the life force; and it also sounded more like a woman's name than a man's. For a period of time, my prayers began with Dear Via and ended with Amen. When I named God "Via," I didn't know that the Canadian public railroad service was also commonly called "Via," short for Via Rail. If I'd known that, I might have chosen another name, or I might not. Praying is both a private and a public transportation system; I might have enjoyed the connection.

When I prayed to Via, I pictured God as a woman in the prime of life. She had long, dark hair and wore a robe that flowed out around her, with the sun, the moon, and the stars woven through it. Her arms were outstretched. My prayers during this time were very simple. I asked Via to be with those I loved, including myself. I named people and asked Via to be with them. Sometimes I said, "Via, hold Edythe [or whoever] in your arms. Give her a moment of rest and peace." I'd say that last part especially if the person were ill, or if I knew the person were in some kind of trouble. My Grandmother Scott—my mother's mother—declined and died during this period, and I often asked Via to hold my grandmother in her arms.

In one way I felt odd praying to Via for my grandmother. A pastor's widow, Grandmother Scott once told me that it was a big mistake for the church to pay attention to the people who wanted to argue about God's gender. She told me emphatically that God's gender was male, that this was *true*, and therefore any other representation of God was *false*. She was upset after a Methodist general convention in which people raised the issue of changing the Methodist liturgy so that God wasn't so insistently male all the time. She thought that even by discussing the matter, church leaders were going to hell in a hand basket, though she wouldn't have put it that way. A little part of me felt guilty about praying to Via, a female God, for my grandmother. But most of me felt fine about it.

In time, the list of people in my prayers expanded to include people I didn't know. I'd pray for Via to be with everyone in my town, whoever they were. Everyone in my state. Everyone in the world. In this process I discovered a paradox about praying for other people. The paradox helped me with one of my own spiritual problems—the feeling of fragmentation and disconnection that sometimes plagued me.

If I started my prayer by asking Via to be with me, and then with my husband David, and gradually worked my way outward, including the other people I loved—naming them—and then the people in my town, until finally I asked Via to be with all living beings, by the end of the prayer I was able to find my own place in the list. By the end of the prayer, I had a solid internal awareness of myself as a member of all living beings. With this awareness came a moment of peace.

I've told my women friends about this stage in my prayer life, when I switched my image of God from male to female, and a surprising number of them said, "Oh yes, I did that too." Women both inside and outside traditional religious organizations, sometimes without telling anyone, begin to pray to a female image of God. Like me, those I talked to found it to be a step forward. It broke the hold of the male God on their minds. Praying to a female God expanded their idea of what God could be. Some of the women I talked to still pray to a female God. But even though God became more all-encompassing for me through this exercise, gradually, as I prayed to Via, I realized that my underlying problem remained unsolved.

A female God lacks some of the limitations of a male God, but in her own way, she's no less limited. I wondered if maybe the heart of the problem wasn't even gender, but the human image. I couldn't separate human qualities—love, thought, intention, and purposeful action—from the human image in my mind. And these were the qualities that I couldn't be sure my God had.

An unintentional God

I stopped saying Dear Via and started saying Dear God again around the same time that I first dropped in on the Unitarians and the Episcopalians. At church, of course, I was surrounded by images of God, most of them anthropomorphic and male. We Unitarians at the Quimper Fellowship did experience some non-male images of God. We heard a children's story from Africa in which God was a woman wearing a two-toned hat. We watched a Buddhist parable in which the Buddha was portrayed by two children, one male, one female. But it seemed to me that we Unitarians held our images of God at arm's length, to be learned from, but not prayed to or worshiped. When we Unitarians looked at God, we looked at images from cultures other than our own. The Judeo-Christian God rarely made an appearance.

At St. Paul's, in contrast, the Judeo-Christian God was everywhere, insistent, demanding to be embraced. He was in the window we Episcopalians faced every Sunday, his loving arm around the penitent sinner. He was in the Nicene Creed we recited each week, defined and compartmentalized. He was in the prayers and the scripture readings. We worshipped him in hymns, in canticles, and in the gorgeous hyperbole of the Psalms.

> *The law of the Lord is perfect*
> *and revives the soul;*
> *the testimony of the Lord is sure*
> *and gives wisdom to the innocent.*
> *The statutes of the Lord are just*
> *and rejoice the heart;*
> *the commandment of the Lord is clear*
> *and gives light to the eyes.*
> *The fear of the Lord is clean*
> *and endures for ever;*
> *the judgements of the Lord are true*
> *and righteous altogether.*
> *More to be desired are they than gold,*
> *more than much fine gold,*
> *sweeter far than honey, than honey in the comb.*
> *Psalms 19: 7-10*

In retrospect, it was a good thing I'd made some headway on the male/female problem of God before returning to church. I had enough trouble coming to terms with a perfect Creator-Ruler-Judge without having to argue with myself over gender, too. For the most part I successfully ignored the overwhelming maleness of God at St.

Paul's. When I couldn't ignore it, I did my best to forgive it. I told myself that the *language* had gotten stuck in the Father/Son metaphor. *I* hadn't.

I needed to save my energy for the rest of it—a God who was both just and merciful. A God who had written perfect law. A God who knew the score. This was the God I encountered at St. Paul's from 10:00 to 11:15 every other Sunday morning. Then I walked out of the red arched doors and faced God's unjust and imperfect creation.

One day shortly after David and I moved into our house, we were fixing lunch together in the kitchen when a small object slammed into the kitchen window, shaking the pane. We were shocked at the force of the blow and had no idea what made it. I remember feeling my heart in my mouth. We ran outside. A pine sisken, a gray and yellow finch-like bird, lay on the gravel beneath the window, panting and shaking. We felt terrible but didn't know what to do to help the bird. We debated on whether to pick it up and put it in a more sheltered spot or leave it alone to find its own wits, finally deciding to leave it alone. Twenty minutes later, it was gone, and we were relieved.

Then the following day, it all happened again—the sharp impact, the pine sisken on the ground. This time, broken neck. The bird was dead. Standing in bewilderment beside its carcass—Why would this happen two days in a row?—I looked up at the window and saw the answer. The angle of sunlight had turned our south-facing windows into mirrors, perfectly reflecting the woods around the house. The bird must have hit the window at full speed, believing it was flying into the woods rather than against a house. No wonder it broke its neck.

After that day, I checked the reflection off our south-facing windows in all seasons and all weather. Most times and most days, the windows look like windows, not mirrors, and no bird is dumb enough to fly into them. But occasionally, for an hour or so, they turn into mirrors. When they do, they're deadly.

David and I have mulled over this problem, but a solution hasn't come easily. Our south-facing windows provide us with light and a view of the woods. We haven't yet figured out how to alert the birds to the windows during those minutes when they need alerting, without obscuring our light and view all the rest of the time. We feel responsible for creating the hazard, and I hope we'll come up with a solution eventually. In the meantime, living in a woods has given me some perspective on the problem that might not have been visible in a more human-dominated, urban environment. While we humans sometimes recognize and take responsibility for the hazards we create, who takes responsibility for all the rest of the much greater and more common hazards in God's creation?

Few plants or animals in the forest die in peaceful old age. The woods is built on the carcasses of plants that took root at the wrong spot and animals that ran or flew the wrong way at the wrong time. Our house is a human contribution to this pattern. It isn't fair. It isn't just. But it isn't unnatural, either, and it isn't the lone injustice of the forest. After attending a church service at St. Paul's, I would look at the reflection off our house's windows, or at a tree blown down in a storm, or at a half-eaten field mouse at the edge of the drain field, and ask myself: *Why do we put a just and loving God at the heart of an unjust universe?*

The way I saw it, the universe exists by way of random events, whether they cause suffering or joy. The life we see around us appears to be the result of foresight and intelligence only because it is so intricate. In fact, this very intricacy is the natural result of a long chain of evolutionary accidents that happened to be capable of reproducing themselves. Life looks as good as it does because the other accidents, the vast majority that couldn't reproduce themselves, fell away. We see the result of a small fraction of the billions of accidents that have occurred—those few that survived to make us.

One summer day, my eight-year-old nephew Max, eating lunch in front of the television at his home near the east coast of Australia, tried to swallow a whole cherry tomato and failed. The tomato lodged in his throat. He couldn't breathe or speak. He was alone in the family room. Max walked into my sister Rose's office and stood looking at her. "What?" she said. He couldn't answer. In a few seconds, he lost consciousness and collapsed on the floor. Rose called an ambulance. Paramedics rushed Max to a hospital. The tomato was dislodged in time and he recovered completely. Every day, other children, as well as adults, choke to death while eating.

That anecdote isn't about unfairness alone, it's also about God's questionable engineering skills. If a God deliberately designed us, then we humans choke on our food *by design*. Would a competent engineer design the human body so that the eating tube shares a section with the breathing tube? This feature in our design survives for a simple reason: choking to death on food doesn't kill enough of us. Enough of us manage to both eat and breath throughout our lives so the design feature gets passed from generation to generation. As a result, some members of each generation choke to death while eating, and those who love them mourn.

Trying to figure out who I was praying to when I said "Dear God," I got tied up in knots between what I thought God had to be and what I saw the universe to be. In my mind, the idea of God was inextricably linked to the idea of purpose and plan in the universe. At St. Paul's, we worshiped a God who created the universe, who was slow to anger, who was just, and who loved us. The problem with these descriptions was that when I compared them to the world as I perceived it—an inherently unjust world—they made me so angry, I couldn't see straight. I couldn't see through them to whatever God might be for me. I wanted to know what I was praying to, and the only answer that came back was some variation of "not *that*!"

Finally, I decided to go with "not *that!*" and see where it took me. I began to strip away what I had thought of as God's characteristics.

If the problem was gender, then take it away. The God who received my prayers was not gendered any more than the stars are gendered. That characteristic fell away without a moment's regret on my part.

If the problem was personality—human personality with human values and emotions—then take it away. The phrases "God is just" or "God is love" might mean something, but they didn't mean that God was fair and loved me the way my father was fair and loved me. When the human characteristics fell away, they left question marks behind. I was much more confident about stripping God of gender than I was about stripping God of love. I left the question marks in place for the time being. But for now, my God was devoid of personality.

If the problem was intention and purpose, then take them away. My God had never intended, decided, nor acted with any purpose whatsoever.

But what was left? Could I really strip away intention and still have God? Was I back to nothing at all?

It felt that way at first, but in fact, stripping away God's characteristics helped me get down to the basics. It was around this time that I started going to the spiritual discussion group in my rector's home and eventually wrote the prayer that starts, *"Dear God, who made the rocks just the way they are, rising from the earth."* Besides helping me figure out how to love a fellow group member, that prayer also showed me something I thought was true about God. The prayer is really a list of things in creation—rocks, stars, wind, water, deer, moles, and people. Each item in the list is described as being just the way it is . . . in a state of some kind of change.

My God made things. Having made them, God caused things to

change. Maybe God made things with change in their very nature. Either way, I prayed to whatever it was that caused things to be in a universe in which everything is constantly transforming into something else.

Did I pray to . . . the laws of physics and chaos? Not the human approximations of those laws that we write in textbooks, but the real laws, independent of our definitions, that drive existence forward. If I prayed for perspective greater than my own and other than my own, for perspective that existed before me and will exist after me, then maybe I prayed to the force of gravity, or to the hydrogen atom, or to energy and light. Was that it?

Yes, in a way.

I never felt closer to God than when I turned my compost pile. Forking over the compost, smelling the dark, sweet material, looking close to see the material come alive and move, a worm shining in sunlight, a millipede crawling toward shadow, a slug burrowing into a grapefruit rind. The sense of awe, the strange mix of pride and humility that filled me. What did I pray to? Was I praying to the source of that awe?

Yes, in a way.

I prayed to what all things hold in common. I prayed to what makes life. I thought about the elements of the universe, the rocks, the stars, the air, other living things. I tried to get the perspective of what's behind all that. I prayed to the force that brings things into existence. I thought this force encompassed all it created. My God was transcendent, and my God was also immanent. God ran in my veins. God lived and died and lived again in every atom of the universe.

When I prayed, I tried to feel that I was part of God, and God was a part of me. Through that feeling, I tried to grasp what I could do, how I could change to make a whole life, a good life.

By stripping away God's personality, I had revealed what was essential to me about God. God was no longer a blank. God made all things, caused all things to change into other things, and inhabited all things.

Everything else about God was a mystery. I could live with that mystery.

Dressing the emperor

Once I saw God as being beyond human characteristics or personality to speak of, and I was reconciled to the mystery of God's nature, then something new happened. I began to see God from a new perspective. It was as if I'd been traveling along the curves of a spiral, come around a turn, and seen a side of the center I'd seen before, long ago, when I was on another curve. This time around, though, it looked different. Finally, I began to forgive images of God for their limitations and contradictions.

It's hard to talk about God. And when you strip away personality and characteristics, it gets a lot harder. After struggling to be coherent about something that is, in its essence, a mystery, it occurred to me that religions were just trying to put a bit of clothing on the unknowable, so that we could see a shape and talk about it. Shiva, the Buddha, the Trinity, the great web of being—all these images were metaphors for what is truly unspeakable. All religions use substitute names for God, and we get in serious trouble when we think we're using the real name. I had mistaken the clothing that religions put on their Gods for the God that animates the robes.

It isn't that God is a human creation, any more than gravity is a human creation. Our definitions of God are human creations, though, just as our definitions of gravity are human creations. Our attempts to describe gravity are flawed not only because we still have things to learn about gravity, but also because we can only perceive gravity through our human mind and senses. We'll always know only a human *idea* of gravity and not gravity itself.

Once I saw God in this light, the outfits that people put on God began to look less stupid and more useful. The Hebrew God, who had repelled me all the time I was an atheist outside the church, turned out to be a surprisingly accurate human representation of the forces of creation and fate: arbitrary and powerful; by turns just, unjust, nurturing, vengeful, forgiving, and unforgiving; and above all, always with us. I was still mad at the guy, but at least I had some glimmering of how he got his reputation.

I started to keep a nature diary. It seemed to me a direct adjunct to my prayer life. Two or three times a week I wrote a short, detailed description of something currently happening in nature near my house. A cloud bank pouring across the sky from the southwest. Bracken uncurling. The sound of a snake moving from the warm gravel beside the lane into the underbrush at the edge of the forest. At first I tried to write the descriptions from memory at my desk, but that wasn't *good* enough. I took my notebook out with me, or brought a twig or leaf inside. I bought field guides to learn the names of the things I described. The dichotomy I had seen between science and religion, between rationality and belief, broke down. It was all religion. Paying attention to the natural world around me, listening to a talk on the historical Jesus at the Quimper Fellowship with my fellow Unitarians, singing the Gloria at St. Paul's with my fellow Episcopalians: it was all religion.

I even came to terms with the primary descriptions of God used at both my churches, descriptions that had bored and annoyed me when I had first come back to church.

The word "God" rarely appeared in the Unitarian liturgies at Quimper Fellowship. Instead, we used phrases such as "ultimate reality" or "source of all" when referring to God, and at first I had found this extremely annoying. *Ultimate reality.* Whatever *that* is! But after struggling with my own definition of God for a while, those

Unitarian phrases sounded better. I could tell that the people who came up with them weren't just casting about at random for anything that wouldn't offend Unitarian atheists, a prickly crew. They were trying to be accurate. I did think that God was ultimate reality; I just didn't know what that *was*. I did think that God was the source of all. The Unitarian phrases still weren't exactly music to my ears. They weren't art. On the other hand, they weren't trying to be art. They were just trying to be clear, and I respected the effort.

At St. Paul's, it was the Trinity: the Father, Son, and Holy Spirit. When I first returned to Christian churches, I had little use for the Trinity as a description of God. I thought it smacked of committee work. A few hundred years after Jesus lived and died, a bunch of clerics got together to describe what was new about God in their young religion. In my judgment, they had compromised on a description that contained a little of what was most important to each of them, without, unfortunately, making much sense. I had seen the same thing happen in software design more than once, so I was familiar with the dynamics. They couldn't quite give up monotheism, but they couldn't quite hang on to it, either. Result: A conundrum that plagued and puzzled Christians from school children to graying theologians ever since. Three in one. A father and a son, distinct and yet joined. A spirit, also distinct, and also joined to both father and son. When I first came back to church, the Trinity didn't do much for me but muddy the waters.

However, just because the features in a software product are designed by compromise doesn't necessarily mean the product is no good. Often, the main point of the compromise is to end up with something that people can apply to real problems before they die of old age waiting for the ultimate product to be released.

So I asked myself, could the Trinity be useful to me? Other aspects of the service at St. Paul's were useful. The prayers helped me say things to God. Even when the words weren't what I would have said on my own, the practice of talking to God with other people, using words that other people had composed, helped me talk to God later by myself. The confession helped me face up to my shortcomings. The bread and wine helped me recognize a direct encounter with God when I had one. But what about the Trinity? If I couldn't use the Trinity, much of the language and imagery in the church were also useless to me.

During Pentecost season, which lasts from the end of May until the end of November, a white stained-glass dove hangs in front of the sanctuary at St. Paul's. In Christian imagery, a white dove represents the Holy Spirit, which descended to Jesus at his baptism in the form of a dove and to the disciples on the day of Pentecost in the form of tongues of fire. The glass dove hangs in full view of the congregation throughout the season of Pentecost as a reminder of the Holy Spirit at work in our lives.

If the Holy Spirit were useless to me as a metaphor for God, then the glass dove was useless as a metaphor for the Holy Spirit, no more than a pretty thing to look at during the sermon. I'm all for pretty things to look at during the sermon—the more the better. But I go to church to get closer to God. Could this glass dove help? Symbol and metaphor can be powerful tools. In addition to the glass dove, hundreds of other Trinitarian images in one form or another pass through St. Paul's during the liturgical year. Could *any* of them help? Or were they all just distractions?

I thought of the language of the Trinity as clothing. How did that language look draped over my God?

The Unitarian words—ultimate reality, source of all—looked okay on my God, if a bit spare. They were about as close to a birthday suit as words for God could be. They fit okay, but there weren't many places I could go with them.

In contrast, the Trinity had the feeling of a costume party, of playing dress-up from a trunk in the attic. Plenty of material here, plenty of folds, drapes, tucks, and hems to cover God's nakedness. At first, I couldn't see much underneath those voluminous church robes. I had to listen to the language awhile, let it go through its variations, and then ask myself: *Could these words represent anything about my God?* Gradually, patterns emerged. The language didn't always fit, but at times I did glimpse movement behind the robes. At times, when artfully presented, the costume of the Trinity could provide a way for me to relate to God.

God the Father, the Creator, was easiest. My God was certainly whatever caused creation, and language about the Father was often tied directly to the creative force. Okay, when I prayed, I was praying to the creative force. With that in mind, I could hear words that referred to the Father and sense what was underneath them for me. And when I did that, I could reach beyond the father image and grasp the life-giving force that gave birth to all creation.

At first, I was mystified by the Holy Spirit. I knew the stories of Jesus' baptism and the disciples' encounter with the Holy Spirit at Pentecost, but I had a hard time relating them to my experience of God. After listening to the language about the Holy Spirit in the liturgy for awhile, eventually I did hear patterns that struck a chord. The Holy Spirit was often connected to God's presence, God's *spirit* that suffused creation. Okay. When I prayed, I prayed to a God who was *right here*, not far off looking down at me. I could use the Holy Spirit as a metaphor for God's immanence. Seen in that light, the white glass dove hanging in front of the sanctuary throughout the Pentecost season could hold not only beauty for me, but also meaning.

It was hardest relating Christ, the Son, to my God. For the longest time, I couldn't find a pattern in the language surrounding Jesus Christ that worked—for me, there was too much language pointing in too many directions. Over the centuries, as Christianity has built up the Jesus image, it has became all things for all people. I had to dig deep into the language to find whatever meaning it could have for me. Eventually, I got a clue from a puzzling phrase in the Nicene Creed that refers to Jesus Christ: *"Through him all things were made."*

Since many things were made before Jesus was born, clearly, this sentence was talking about the eternal Christ rather than the human being, Jesus of Nazareth. The Creed had already described the Father as *"maker of heaven and earth, of all that is, seen and unseen."* And yet, here it said that all things were made through Christ. For many months, that sentence meant nothing to me. I figured it was just the guys in Nicaea trying to jack up Jesus' image in some inexplicable way. However, as my ideas about my own God became more clear, I finally saw an association between the two.

I don't know much about how things were made in the very beginning, but I know how things are made now. They're made from other things. I'm made from what came before me, and I will provide the makings for what comes next. All things are made *through transformation*. Christ—the Son—could be, at least in part, a metaphor for the cycle of birth, death, and rebirth into something new. When I prayed, I prayed both to and for transformation. Once I related Christ to the idea of, and hope for, transformation, more of the language about him worked for me. For example, at the end of almost all Episcopal prayers, we say that we pray "through Jesus Christ our Lord," or "through Jesus Christ our Savior." I had always thought of those endings as boilerplate. Now, it made perfect sense to me to pray to God through Christ.

In this way, I came to terms with the Trinity. It was a long, confusing, sometimes scary process. Scary, because of the possibility that I was just talking myself into it. I *like* symbol and metaphor. I *wanted* those images and metaphors to work for me, and knowing that I wanted them to work, I was suspicious when they did. Was I rationalizing my view of the world to fit in with the other people in the pews? Twisting the words and images of Christianity so that I could listen to them, say them, and convince myself that I wasn't a hypocrite? Sometimes, the answer to those questions seemed to be yes. Those were the most frightening times of the whole process.

However, I knew that wanting the glass dove to have meaning, trying to find a connection between its Christian meaning and my understanding of God, then using the image as a medium to get to God, were not necessarily the actions of an intellectual fraud. It was a balancing act. As it happens, I don't have very good balance—my father sweated through three long summers teaching me how to ride a bike before I finally got it, and I'm not much use on a ladder today. I often felt, as I came to terms with the Trinity, that I was teetering on the high wire of intellectual integrity, nearly falling in one direction or the other. All I could do was try to be aware of it, and try to hang on.

Much if not most of the language relating to God in the Christian church still gave me pause. All the terms describing God in a morally positive light remained question marks, empty phrases that did not, as far as I could tell, describe my God. *"God of justice." "God of peace."* Wishful thinking, I believed. However, once I could relate to the basic metaphors for God in the Christian church, I could use the stories and myths of Christianity as tools to help me develop my relationship with God.

And if I liked metaphor, I loved story even more.

"The Harbor Bell"
by John H. Yates

Verse 1:
Our life is like a stormy sea
Swept by the gales of sin and grief,
While on the windward and the lee
Hang heavy clouds of unbelief;
But o'er the deep a call we hear,
Like harbor bells' inviting voice;
It tells the lost that hope is near,
And bids the trembling soul rejoice.

Chorus:
This way, this way,
O heart oppressed,
So long by storm
and tempest driv'n;
This way, this way,
lo here is rest,
Rings out the harbor bells
of heaven.

Verse 2:
O let us now the call obey,
And steer our bark for yonder shore,
Where still that voice directs the way,
In pleading tones for ever more;

A thousand life wrecks strew the sea;
They're going down at ev'ry swell;
"Come unto me, Come unto me,"
Rings out th' assuring harbor bell.

Verse 3:
O tempted one, look up, be strong;
The promise of the Lord is sure,
That they shall sing the victor's song,
Who faithful to the end endure;
God's Holy Spirit comes to thee,
Of his abiding love to tell;
To blissful port, o'er story sea,
Calls heav'ns inviting harbor bell.

Verse 4:
Come, gracious Lord, and in thy love
Conduct us o'er life's stormy wave;
O guide us to the home above,
The blissful home beyond the grave;
There safe from rock, and storm,
    and flood,
Our song of praise shall never cease,
To Him who bought us with His blood,
And brought us to the port of peace.

Chapter VIII

Grappling with Myth

High in the tower of St. Paul's Episcopal church in Port Townsend hangs a brass bell with a curious history. As the story goes, one foggy evening in the 1870s, a sailing vessel approached Port Townsend with a famous gospel singer standing on its deck. The singer's name was Ira D. Sankey, and he performed in world-wide revival tours with evangelist Dwight Moody. Sankey was traveling from Victoria to a singing engagement in Seattle. In the dense fog that night, his vessel lost its bearings and was threatened with destruction on the rocks of Port Townsend Bay. The captain ordered the distress whistle blown, and in reply came the sound of a bell from shore—St. Paul's church bell, rung by parishioners to help the lost ship find the harbor. Guided by the bell, the vessel made it to safety. Sankey was so inspired by his ship's deliverance, he wrote a hymn about it as he made his way from Port Townsend to Seattle. He named the hymn "The Harbor Bell" and sang it in Seattle to great acclaim. The words to the hymn use the call of the harbor bell, bringing a ship through the fog into safety, as a metaphor for the Holy Spirit calling the human soul to spiritual safe harbor.

"The Harbor Bell" became a hit in port towns around the world through the turn of the century. Sankey sang it at Moody's revival meetings, and it was sung at Sunday morning services from Boston to London, including at St. Paul's Episcopal church in Port Townsend, Washington. The parishioners, proud to own the bell that inspired such a famous hymn, sang it every year on the parish anniversary.

I know the story of the bell and the hymn because a few months after I joined St. Paul's, I was asked to help update the parish history for their 135th anniversary. In my research, I read the story of the bell and the hymn in virtually every previous rendering of the parish history. It was practically scripture. However, like much scripture, its source was hard to pin down: many people knew the story, but no one could tell me where it originated. Facts and dates changed between accounts. One account even had the same voyage inspiring two sets of verses: the hymn by Sankey and a different poem by an unnamed passenger on the same ship. I wasn't sure which version of the story to use in the updated history.

Finally, in the back of an old file I discovered a note typed in the 1940s and saved by a vicar of St. Paul's who evidently found the story as curious as I did. The note quoted from Sankey's own published autobiography, telling how the "The Harbor Bell" was written. As I read, the dearly held legend cracked apart.

Ira Sankey wrote music, not lyrics. The lyrics to "The Harbor Bell" were written by a man named John Yates, who sent them to Sankey in 1891. Yates told Sankey he was inspired, not by being saved in the fog outside Port Townsend, but by a newspaper article that described how a ship was saved in heavy fog by a harbor bell. Yates didn't name the harbor or even say that the bell was a church bell. It could have been St. Paul's bell—or any other bell in any foggy port town.

In the same file I found a hand-written account by an early member of St. Paul's who told of the steamer Eliza Anderson, lost in dense fog, guided to port by the ringing of St. Paul's church bell. An unnamed passenger on the steamer wrote a poem about the experience called "The Church Fog Bell," which was also in the file. This incident occurred in September, 1868, more than twenty years before John Yates sent his lyrics to Ira Sankey.

I wondered if Yates, the author of "The Harbor Bell," could possibly have seen the poem in the church journal before he wrote his lyrics. If he did, then St. Paul's bell may have inspired the famous hymn at some distance. The possibility seemed remote: twenty years passed between the poem's publication and the appearance of Yates' lyrics. But it was worth a check. I compared the two pieces. They shared themes that might have occurred to any religious writer who wrote about a bell saving a ship in the fog, but weren't much alike in approach and language. I doubted if one had influenced the other.

As I puzzled over the old documents, it sank into me that the claim that St. Paul's bell had saved a famous man's life and inspired a famous hymn was most likely a fabrication . . . a lie that caught people's fancy and was repeated many times. One of the most oft-told stories of the parish was all fiction. I started to feel like an investigative reporter with a big scoop. I didn't have to choose which version of the story to tell; instead, I could expose it as a fraud. I imagined deleting all references to "The Harbor Bell" from the updated history, then laying out the facts in an extended footnote, to the stunned admiration of all who read it.

Then I imagined St. Paul's long-time parishioners reading their updated history. I had interviewed some of these people as part of my research and respected their work in the parish. Many of them could still remember singing "The Harbor Bell" every year on the parish anniversary. I doubted if "stunned admiration" was quite the term to describe their emotion on seeing their history rewritten by a relative stranger. I began to feel less like an investigative reporter and more like a ship approaching rocky shoals in the fog.

In this state of doubt, I turned to whatever I could say about the bell that seemed to be true. As I wrote and rewrote, my feelings about the legend of the bell and the hymn changed. Its most commonly told "facts"—that Ira Sankey wrote "The Harbor Bell" after his life was saved in Port Townsend harbor by St. Paul's church bell—were completely untrue. Still, the legend contained ghosts of real historical and spiritual events, and I began to see it as containing its own kind of truth.

St. Paul's bell saved lives, no doubt about that. The bell was presented to the church by a local ship captain with the understanding it would be rung during foggy weather so ships could find the harbor. The steamer Eliza Anderson would not have been the only ship guided to harbor by its peals. Many early residents of Port Townsend knew the harrowing experience of being guided through the shoals on no more than the ringing of a church bell. Both lives and property were at stake: the folks on those ships would have had no trouble comparing their church bell to the Holy Spirit calling a lost soul home.

One of the definitions of the word *myth* in the American Heritage Dictionary is "a story, a theme, an object, or a character, regarded as embodying an aspect of a culture." The words to "The Harbor Bell" certainly expressed an aspect of Port Townsend culture, and the parish already had a twenty-year-old story of a saved ship and an inspired poem. When the members of St. Paul's claimed the famous hymn's bell as their own, they were connecting their experience to something beyond the city limits, linking their physical and spiritual peril to people in port towns everywhere. It wasn't Ira Sankey on that ship; it was the townspeople themselves. Sankey's hymn expressed what was in their own hearts so clearly, they simply placed him beside them on the fog-bound deck. The elements of the story—the saved ship, the inspired passenger—were revised and then retold a hundred times because the spiritual truth of the revised story spoke more powerfully to the people in the town than the facts.

The story of St. Paul's bell and the famous hymn wasn't a lie. It was a myth. A small, local myth.

So what does the writer of parish history do with a small, local myth? I had lost all interest in debunking this legend. By the time I came to write the final draft of St. Paul's history, what was false about the story of the bell and the hymn was less interesting than what was true about the myth. On the other hand, I was trying in the parish history to say, in all good faith, what had actually occurred.

Finally, I included what seemed to be true about the bell—the captain's gift, the saved ships, the locally inspired poem. Without going into details, I added that the bell was also *said* to have inspired the words to the famous hymn "The Harbor Bell," which was certainly true. It had been said again and again. I made sure that the parish historical files retained facts known about the hymn's composition, in case anyone was curious enough to look them up, and explained to the historical committee why the whole story didn't appear in the updated history. To my surprise, the committee didn't seem particularly concerned about it, even though more than one of them had told me the story themselves. Its fabricated details fell away from the parish history without a ripple.

In retrospect, I understood better why the story could drop away so easily. St. Paul's bell no longer rang out as warning to ships in the fog; instead, the Coast Guard maintained a lighthouse with a piercing foghorn. Any large vessel in the harbor would have its own sounding devices onboard. The parish had even stopped singing the hymn on its anniversary some years earlier with few complaints from the parishioners. Though people liked the old story, it no longer spoke to them personally. The myth had outlived its usefulness, and it turned out to be my job not to explode it, but simply to let it die a natural death.

Rewriting scripture

Once I knew the facts, or what facts could be known, about St. Paul's bell, those facts helped me understand and appreciate the myth of St. Paul's bell. It also helped, I think, that I had some distance from it; it wasn't *my* myth. Myths that strike closer to home—those that formed our own culture, and in some cases are still alive in our culture—can be harder to befriend. In the months that followed my return to church, I often wished that a few Judeo-Christian myths would fall away as easily as the myth of the church bell and the hymn. I could have done without the stories of Jesus's miracles: making the blind see, feeding thousands with a few loaves and fishes, bringing the dead to life. Or the supernatural events that God engineered for the Hebrew people: creepy plagues climaxing in the deaths of firstborn children, food raining down from the sky, the sun standing still to prolong a bloody victory. Those stories seemed like propaganda; they smelt of fireworks and fairy dust. Part of the problem was that questions of historical accuracy can be so loud and distracting in the Christian church, which makes it hard to get in the myths' wavelength. I'd be caught up in the physical impossibility of a virgin birth, for example, and as long as I was arguing with myself—or with my mental projection of the person sitting next to me in the pew—about whether Mary could have been a virgin, I was distracted from any meaning the story might have for me.

One Sunday at the Quimper Unitarian Fellowship, our guest speaker described *The Jefferson Bible* in her talk, and I thought it sounded like just the ticket. *The Jefferson Bible* is a version of the four gospels edited by Thomas Jefferson, the third President of the United States. As I had learned from Unitarian pamphlets, Jefferson was a prominent Unitarian in his time, and—as I learned from an Episcopal priest—he also sat on the vestry of his home Episcopal parish. So I thought Jefferson and I had at least a little in common. When I heard his approach to Bible reading, he seemed like a kindred soul. Jefferson took a scalpel to his copy of the Gospels, clipped all of Jesus' non-miraculous acts and words of wisdom, then pasted them in order on blank sheets of paper. In this way, he created a version of the gospels that contained no supernatural acts. An edition of his work called *The Jefferson Bible* is published by Beacon Press. I ordered a copy from the U.U. bookstore in Boston and read it as soon as it came. Jesus' voice is one of the best things in the New Testament: confident, crafty, witty, blunt to rudeness and beyond, issuing challenges as hard to evade as they are to face. With most of the other stuff cut away, Jefferson's edited version of the gospels was a short, exhilarating ride. It ended up on my nightstand instead of any of the translations of the Bible approved by the Episcopal church. To Jefferson, the wisdom of Jesus' words told the true story of Christianity, and I agreed with him.

Given a free hand, I would have happily rewritten a lot more of the Bible than Jefferson did. Surely something could be done about the overwhelming maleness of it all—Noah, Abraham, Isaac, Moses, Jesus, Peter, Paul. Women do appear in the Bible, but we rarely get to be main characters. I thought it would be a good idea to rewrite the whole shebang, reversing the gender of all characters, major and minor. Starting at the top. How about a search-and-replace that changed each pronoun referring to God from "he" to "she"? How about a female Moses negotiating with a female Pharaoh? Twelve female disciples and a male hanger-on named Marvin Magdalene? Some of the stories could be easily changed with nothing more than new names and pronouns; others would require careful and inspired writing to make them work with the genders reversed. As a writer, I thought it sounded like a lot of fun.

Then what to do with the new version? This particular God had been a "he" for at least five thousand years. It seemed excessive to ask for equal time . . . I thought just five *hundred* years of payback would be enough. We'd use the new, female-dominated version of the Bible exclusively in all churches, say, for half a millennium, then resurrect the old, male-dominated version and trade off, maybe every other Sunday.

I had fun just thinking about it. In the meantime, every other Sunday, I encountered that old, male-dominated version at St. Paul's. We heard a passage from the Hebrew Bible or the Christian

Apocrypha, sang a Psalm, then heard a passage from the Epistles and one from the Gospels. Then the sermon, usually inspired by the Gospel reading. Two Sundays a month, I heard it the way it was. Then I heard commentary on the way it was.

Through months of services, it was brought home to me that the images of God in the Bible were not as relentlessly male as I had thought. The image of God as bread, as a woman giving birth, as fire, as the breath of life, as a mother eagle in the nest, as a father, a son, a bridegroom, as a shepherd, as a lamb, as a mountain—all these and more appeared in the Bible passages I heard in church. Some books in the Hebrew Bible and Christian Apocrypha also referred to a companion of God called Wisdom. Wisdom is always "she," because the word for Wisdom in Hebrew is a feminine noun. Wisdom doesn't get as much ink as God Himself, but still, there she was. I read some Christian theology suggesting that the Holy Spirit was the Christian incarnation of Wisdom and should also be referred to as "she." The Judeo-Christian God wasn't as narrowly defined as I thought.

Wisdom praises herself, and tells of her glory in the midst of her people. In the assembly of the Most High she opens her mouth, and in the presence of his hosts she tells of her glory: "I came forth from the mouth of the Most High, and covered the earth like a mist . . . Over waves of the sea, over all the earth, and over every people and nation I have held sway . . . Come to me, you who desire me, and eat your fill of my fruits. For the memory of me is sweeter than honey, and the possession of me sweeter than the honeycomb. Those who eat of me will hunger for more, and those who drink of me will thirst for more. Whoever obeys me will not be put to shame, and those who work with me will not sin.

—Sirach 24:1-6, 19-22 (Sirach is an Apocryphal book of the Bible.)

The God who appeared in our weekly scripture readings at St. Paul's was still almost always a guy, and when we prayed, we usually prayed to the Father. I would have preferred more variety, particularly more gender variety, in the images of God I encountered at church. However, the sprinkling of other-than-male images that did appear through the texts leavened the problem a bit.

Besides demonstrating that I couldn't change God's gender with a simple search-and-replace from "he" to "she," those weekly scripture readings gave me another reason to think twice about rewriting the Bible: I admired some of the writing too much to mess with it. Many different people wrote the Bible; some were more skilled than others. Not every chapter in the Bible is good writing. But at its best, it's perfect. When the writing is good, it is so good that I knew I would be the greatest fool in Christendom to fiddle with it. Rewrite the Book of Job to suit my own gender sensibilities? Add my editorial wisdom to the wisdom of Ecclesiastes? I thought it'd be better to leave well enough alone.

During this time, I also read some of the outpouring of contemporary biblical scholarship. I was lucky at this stage to be living in a great age of biblical scholarship. Archeological discoveries this century have shed new light on the life and times of the first Christians. Modern techniques of close textual analysis have revealed more about the composition of the Bible than has been known since the words were first written down. And after millennia of suppression, in the last hundred years, serious scholars have had the opportunity to work on the question of how and when the Bible was written, and then, miracle of miracles, to publish their work. You could say that the established Church finally allowed this work to be published, or you could say it lost its power to suppress it. Either way, new information and theories pour forth, at last.

Contemporary biblical scholarship does its best to set the sto-

ries of the Bible in the time and place of their first telling. It shows
the authors of the Bible struggling to tell the story of how their people
came to God, and how God came to them. Like the story of St. Paul's
bell and the famous hymn, many Bible stories grew out of real events:
their meaning is bound to particular times, places, and incidents that
changed the way people defined themselves and their relationship to
God. In some cases, the authors of the Bible re-told stories that were
already ancient in their time. In others, the authors took contemporary or near-contemporary events and added, subtracted, or rear-
ranged details to help people perceive the meaning and importance
of the events. The writers were both constricted and freed by the
story-telling conventions of their time, just as we are constricted and
freed by our own, different conventions. For better or worse, the results of their labor became Holy Scripture: religious stories created
to make sense of real events. The problem with rewriting these stories to suit my preferences was that I would corrupt their truth in trying to find my own. I became convinced, reluctantly, that rewriting
those stories to satisfy my own turn-of-the-millennium sensibilities
would be a kind of rape.

Becoming human with Adam and Eve

Stories in the Bible became more interesting to me after I realized they were trying to get at something other than historical fact.
Before this, I had thought of Bible stories in one of two ways. Either I
"believed" in a story, meaning I thought it was based on a historical
event ... or I *didn't* believe in it, in which case it was untrue and ir-
relevant—only a myth.

Now I was on a different wavelength. Could these stories be part
of *my* myth? The actual historical events were still important; they
were important as seeds for the myths. The people who wrote the Bi-

ble were trying to come to terms with real events in real lives. Because great myths have meaning across specific events, eras, and cultures, I became interested in the stories of the Bible not only for information about how a particular people related to God, but also, possibly, for information about me, how I related to God and to my world.

For example, when I looked at the biblical account of Adam and Eve not as real or false history, but as a story used to illustrate real events, it unfolded in layers of possible events and meanings.

In one layer, the story was about the transition into consciousness made by the human race at some point in our history. From that perspective, how did the story work? Adam and Eve, tempted by the serpent, chose to go their own way, and the choice was a disaster. Could our species' transition into consciousness possibly have been a choice? Suppose it was ... what would that mean? One or two proto-humans, thousands of years ago, chose to open their eyes to their own actions, observed these actions, reflected on them, and used their reflections to make new choices. The human race stepped onto a new path. The choice turned out to be irreversible. We couldn't go back. And at times, how we long to go back! A simple, unconscious life, just existing every moment without all these constant self-doubts and blundering choices. How beautiful it would be . . . .

. . . Or would it? Would I really give up my consciousness, my awareness of the difference between good and evil, for any prize? Or my ability to choose between them? I can't go back to the Garden of Eden, but is that God's only garden? Maybe there's a path, not back to Eden, but forward to a new life. A path that doesn't require me to give up my all-too-human nature, but embraces it. You could argue that the entire body of Hebrew and Christian scripture is the story of the human search for that path.

In another layer, the story of Adam and Eve might illustrate not an event in the history of the human species, but a passage in the life

of each and every human being—the transition from amoral, innocent infant to conscious and, at times, guilty child.

In yet another layer, the story might illustrate not a single passage in each human life, but a thousand choices we make throughout
our lives: the choice between taking responsibility for an action,
good or evil, and throwing off responsibility to pretend that, whatever
happened, it wasn't our fault. Facing the consequences of our actions
takes us down an extremely painful and arduous road. In the story of
Adam and Eve, this is the first road that the first human beings take.

Liberated by myth

Not all the stories in the Hebrew Bible struck me as being so
rich with possibilities. Some seemed petty and pointless. Others carried a poorly hidden agenda or were so bound in their era's culture
that they barely communicated anything today. But in general, I
could get along with the older Hebrew stories as myth or politicized
history easier than I could get along with the stories in the New Testament. Was the story of Jesus bringing Lazarus to life a myth? What
about the story of Mary and Martha? The Last Supper? It was crucial,
fundamental to Christianity that Jesus was a real human being, and
yet the stories about him in the Gospels seemed to be more about his
divinity than his humanity. I couldn't figure out if they were trying to
give me information about the life of a man, or trying to twist my arm
about his divine nature. It didn't help me that many Christians insisted on the literal truth of the Gospel stories as part of their true
meaning. As a result, the gospel stories put me off. I couldn't find a
way to believe them.

Again I was saved by contemporary scholarship, this time
scholarship I'd heard described as Christianity's death knell. It
came from the Jesus Seminar, a group of academics who made some

waves in New Testament scholarship. They started by analyzing archeological and other historical data of the time, using it to theorize
what kind of teacher Jesus probably was. Then they engaged in close
textual analysis of everything Jesus was supposed to have said in the
Gospels and voted on which sayings were authentic. They ended up
with a mere handful of sentences that they thought Jesus might have
actually said, a tiny minority of everything Jesus was quoted as saying in the gospels. Their conclusions made news. The news made
some people happy and other people mad.

What fascinated me about the Jesus Seminar wasn't their conclusions about what Jesus might have said or might not have said.
Since they made it clear that all they could offer were educated
guesses, their guesses were of academic interest but not much more.
For any given saying, I might vote with them, I might not. But the
more I read the books that fell out of their findings, and other books
that criticized them or developed parallel theories based on historical scholarship, the more a single wonderful fact came through to me.
In a way, I suppose I'd known this fact for a long time, but it made a
big difference to have it stated unequivocally. The fact had to do with
why they could only guess what Jesus really said or did. They were
forced into guessing because, historically speaking, *we know next to
nothing about the events of this guy's life.*

We have more reliable information about St. Paul's bell than we
do about Jesus of Nazareth—much more. We know more about Pontius Pilate and Herod Antipas than we do about Jesus. Pontius Pilate
was the Roman military governor of Judea from 26 to 36 in the Common Era. Herod Antipas was the local ruler of Judea and tetrarch of
Galilee during an overlapping period. Both Roman and Jewish re-
cords say so. Contemporary historians mention their names. Jesus of
Nazareth? *Nada.* The earliest surviving writings that mention Jesus
are letters written by Christian Jews about twenty years after he was
crucified, assuming he was crucified. Crucifixion was a common

form of execution back then and thousands died on crosses, their names and fates unrecorded. The best we can say is that Jesus was probably one of them.

Most of the early letters we have were written by Paul of Tarsus. Paul gives no biographical information about Jesus and doesn't seem to care about it, except to say that Jesus Christ, the Son of God, died on a cross and was raised by God to a new life, which Paul cared about very much indeed. The earliest non-Christian writer to mention Jesus, a Jewish historian named Flavius Josephus, does record that Pilate condemned Jesus to be crucified. However, Josephus wrote in the early 90s, sixty years after the event, and he's known for getting some of his facts wrong. Maybe he was right this time.

The four gospels, written forty to seventy years after Jesus died by Christians who probably had never met him or anybody who knew him personally, contain the earliest biographies of Jesus we have. The authors of the first three gospels wrote close to the time of the fall of Jerusalem to Rome in 73 C.E.; the author of The Gospel of John probably wrote some years later, after the dust had settled.

The gospel writers felt they had been changed, their relationship to their God had been permanently transformed, and they traced the transformation back to a man who had preached in Galilee and Judea before the fall of Jerusalem, a man they called Jesus. They believed he was the Messiah; they called him the Son of God. They believed he would return to establish God's kingdom on earth, and they thought it might happen soon. They sat down and tried to turn his life into a story, to tell other people in their world the good news. Their stories were strongly affected by what was happening right then, in their own lives. The fall of Jerusalem was a pivotal and harrowing event for both the Jewish and Christian people, a number of whom, back then, were the same people. "What does all this mean?" they asked themselves. They wrote about Jesus Christ, and in doing so, like the early people of St. Paul's telling stories about their church bell, the authors of the gospels wrote about themselves. A real man provided the seed for the stories; a real life had been lived. But now I could see that the gospel writers weren't trying to get across the facts of that life so much as the meaning behind the life, the death, and what happened after the death.

I went out and bought an edition of the *New Revised Standard Version* with good notes and a fat concordance. I still liked my *Jefferson Bible*, but now, released from the manacles of fact and pseudo-fact, I was free to look at the stories—the miraculous birth, the healings, walking on water, overcoming death—and ask myself, could this have any meaning for me? Could this story possibly be about me?

Chapter IX

From the Virgin to the Cross

If Mary was a virgin . . .

I distinctly remember a conversation between my brother Brian and me when I was seventeen years old, a senior in high school, and he was thirteen, a freshman. The exchange happened right after the Christmas Eve candlelight service at our family church in Sidney, Ohio. Near the end of the service, Brian and I had stood in our pew next to Mom and Dad, each of us holding a small lighted white candle in a round paper base. My sister, Rose, was up front in the choir. With the rest of the congregation, we all sang the last hymn, "Silent Night, Holy Night":

> *Silent night, holy night,*
> *All is calm, all is bright*
> *Round yon virgin mother and child.*
> *Holy infant so tender and mild,*
> *Sleep in heavenly peace,*
> *Sleep in heavenly peace.*

On the way home after the service, Brian pulled me to one side, out of our parents' earshot, and asked, "If Mary was a virgin, then how did she have a baby?" I don't know at what age, exactly, Mom and Dad unveiled the facts of life to my little brother, but either he had acquired some new information during the past year or he found himself putting two and two together for the first time.

"That's the miracle," I whispered back. "It proves that Jesus is God."

"Ooooooh."

That's how I thought of the virgin birth in those days. It was God doing an impossible thing to prove that Jesus was His son. It was the same as Jesus healing the lepers, raising the dead, making the blind see, turning water into wine and crazy people into sane people, and finally rolling away the stone and walking off into the pre-dawn Judean morning, ready to start a new life. It was all evidence. That stuff was impossible, and only God did impossible things. So Jesus was God.

Twelve months later, a college freshman in a black leotard top and faded Levis, I didn't believe any of it. I didn't think that Mary was technically a virgin when she discovered she was pregnant, that Jesus healed any more effectively than Pastor Bob and his Traveling Gospel Hour, or that a three-day-old corpse had stood up and walked. I wasn't interested in a God who had to work magic tricks to inspire belief. I called myself an agnostic because I didn't want to sound like a know-it-all, but in fact I was an atheist. It took thirty years, until my first Christmas with the Unitarians and the Episcopalians, before I was ready to take another look at the virgin birth.

From one angle, I had been correct in telling my little brother that Mary's virginity proved Jesus' divinity. As I read in my *Interpreter's One-volume Commentary on the Bible*, it was a Hellenic tradition in the ancient world, not a Judaic tradition, for remarkable people to have divine parentage. Alexander the Great, a Greek who lived more than three centuries before Jesus, was also widely reputed to be the product of a virgin birth. And it was a first-century Greek who provided most of the details about Jesus' divine conception, the author of the Gospel of Luke, writing at least seventy years after the fact. Once I knew all that, it seemed obvious that Luke used the idea of a virgin birth to help prove to his fellow Greeks that Jesus was of divine origin.

And yet, the more I read about how religion and myth worked in the lives of early Christians, the more I thought that "proof" wasn't the whole story, or the end of the story. When I saw the virgin birth as proof of Jesus' divinity, I was looking at it through my post-Enlightenment eyes—the only eyes I've got. Nobody in the first century had post-Enlightenment eyes. Back then, hyperbole was a more acceptable literary device than it is today, and stories of divine conception were commonly applied to powerful men, military commanders, or political leaders who changed their world. The big difference in Jesus' case was that the myth got hooked onto a nobody who had been executed by the state for what he said and did. It may be that Luke wasn't saying, "A, and therefore B," so much as he was saying, "Here, where I least expected it, I found the one who changed my world."

Nobody cares how Alexander the Great was conceived anymore, but the conception of Jesus Christ, believed by many to be the living mediator between God and humanity, has been a source of inspiration for two thousand years. Even in today's sex-soaked culture, the virgin birth remains one of the defining images of the Christian church. This was a myth that worked across time and culture; something in it felt true about how humans were reconciled to their divine nature. Whatever the physical facts, Mary's virginity worked for many people on a spiritual level. How come?

For me, the question had changed from this: "How could Mary possibly have been a virgin?" To this: "*Why* a virgin? In bringing God to earth, why did an angel's visitation take the place of the sex act? Could Mary's virginity possibly have anything to do with me?"

When thinking about this, it helped me to forget for a moment the sorrowful Mother of Christ and to picture instead a regular, contemporary virgin. Like me, when I was a virgin. Like the ordinary virgin down the street. The image that came to my mind was of a youth, between 15 and 25 years of age. Either gender would do. A virgin is someone who hasn't done it . . . *yet*. What's dancing around this young innocent, the image that gives the word its *frisson*, is the idea of what's coming, what's right around the corner. The image of the first time.

What will it be like for him? Will she be in love? Will it be fun, or scary, or exciting, or all three? Will he wear a condom? Will she have a good time? Will it be worth it?

A virgin is loaded with potential. Virginity is quite different from passivity, which is the end of retreat. Virginity is the beginning, the moment before the advance. The moment I'm open to receive the divine.

When could God come into me? When I was like a virgin—or as much like a virgin as a middle-aged lady who'd been around the block a few times could be? It wasn't when I thought I knew what I was doing. It wasn't when I'd just done something good. It was more likely to be when I knew I'd screwed up and wanted to make amends: the moment before I picked up the phone, or turned to my spouse, or set out on a long, long walk.

The sex act is just that. An act. Letting God inside doesn't have anything to do with actions. God comes like the angel Gabriel, saying that something is about to happen. Then I decide what to do about it: then I act. God comes when the most important thing about me is not my experience, but my potential; not what I've done, but what I might do. At that moment, I'm a virgin, ripe with possibilities. This is the moment when the door is open and the holy can come into me, and God can be incarnate again on earth.

When I thought about it like that, the Virgin Birth could be a story about me, after all.

Heaven, hell, and the orange peel

When I was a kid, I wanted to go to heaven after I died. More precisely, I didn't want to go to hell. I was afraid of hell, when I

thought about it, which wasn't often. After abandoning organized religion in my late teens, I didn't believe in an afterlife anymore, so I
was no longer afraid of eternal torture at God's command. However,
the loss of hell wasn't a great comfort to me. I was just as afraid to
die—more so, if anything. Instead of going to heaven or hell, I
thought that when you died, everything about you simply stopped being. I believed in the void, and the void has its own terrors.

As I approached the half-century mark of life, I came to another
place. Not a belief in the afterlife, exactly. Also not a belief in the
void, exactly. After seeing the physical and spiritual characteristics
of my parents grow stronger and stronger in me with each passing
year, and after watching the cycles of the seasons in the woods where
we lived, I didn't see death in quite the same way. Between the ages
of twenty and forty, I thought that with death, it was all over. Somewhere in my forties, I started to think that nothing was ever over. It
seemed to me that everything ended up, like my kitchen scraps, in
the compost pile. Compost is never over.

My compost pile is spread across three wooden bins standing in
a row at the border between our yard and the woods. In the first bin,
David and I throw our vegetable and fruit scraps from the kitchen,
weeds from the garden, last year's dead bracken, tree matter from the
rain gutters, and other organic stuff. Sometimes I scrounge a shovelful of manure from a farming neighbor or toss in excess dirt from a
landscape project. The pile in the first bin is colorful with orange and
yellow citrus peels, green broccoli stems, scraps of red pepper and
apple, the ends of carrots, brown and green weeds, and dark dirt.
Slugs glide over it. During three-quarters of the year, a cloud of little
flying insects hovers above it. When the first bin gets full, I take my
pitchfork and turn its contents into the second bin.

The stuff in the second bin is less colorful, more dirt-like, but
still largely recognizable for what it once was. The grapefruit rinds
are faded, slimy, and easy to break apart. Corn cobs no longer have

little bits of corn in them. The dirt that surrounds everything is full of organic matter: twigs, the shredded skeleton of a leaf, a piece of blackened bark. The second bin crawls with earthworms, black-and-yellow millipedes, and gray roly-polies. The mass of material gets smaller as the process goes on, so the second bin is rarely full. I usually turn it into the third bin not because I need the room, but because I want the material for the garden and turning the pile hurries the process along.

Turning the second bin into the third bin is one of my favorite garden tasks. Every pitchfork-full reveals more crawly life. Besides the worms and millipedes, I uncover rough-skinned newts, mottled spiders, and black beetles in the second bin. But the best part is the smell: a sweet, rich odor that makes my head swim with pleasure. The smell of the living earth.

Somehow, turning my compost pile changed the way I viewed my own mortality. As far as I could tell, my compost bins held a microcosm of the processes that rule the universe. Nothing lasts forever, not even empty space. It's filled, then emptied, then filled again. Stones crumble into dust, dust is compacted into bedrock, bedrock is carved into mountains, mountains are beaten down into stones. The orange peel in the first bin does not get to be an orange peel for eternity. By the time I shoveled its atoms out of the third bin and into a hole for a new rhododendron, those atoms weren't orange peel anymore. Some of them would become rhododendron. Others might become dandelion, thistle, or slug. Those I inhaled might spend some time making human cells.

The physical world, at least from my limited perspective, was eternal or as near as made no matter. Whether the universe began with a big bang or a little *phut*, as far as I knew the basic material, the stuff that makes up the atoms, was already there. I didn't know where it came from or how to get rid of it. The orange peel may have stopped existing as an orange peel, but its elements still existed as gases, spider food, or just dirt.

When I rejected the afterlife in my late teens, I did so because it seemed unnatural to me, even blasphemous, to say that human beings escaped death, the fate of all creatures. Instead, it seemed natural to me that when I died, my soul would go out like a burned out light bulb.

Now, after living for nearly fifty years, it seemed *just* as *natural* that my soul would have the same kind of afterlife as the orange peel. Perfectly natural that the soul of one being would be made from the stuff of all souls. When any being died, its soul crumbled and became something entirely different—something new. My soul, my *self*, had been a new creation formed from the compost of what came before me. After I was gone, the heart of me would break apart and make compost for new little hearts.

It was just a way of looking at things. It wasn't harps and flames, and it wasn't the void, either. This way of looking at things didn't reconcile me to death; I still didn't want to die. I doubted if my memory, my perceptions, what I know as my personality would continue after I died. I'm attached to these parts of me and don't want to lose them. I also doubted if I'd join my loved ones beyond the grave in a way that I could recognize while alive. But every time I turned my compost pile, I was convinced that I would join them in some way. Every time that cloud of insects rose above the orange peels, I was convinced that I would rise again.

Even though I still didn't want to die, I lost my sick horror of the void. And if it were true that the spiritual world worked anything like the physical world, then, dear God, I wanted to be the good stuff—black gold, rich, oxygenated, sweet-smelling earth to feed a garden of strong and loving beings.

The cross, the cigarette, and me

If that's the way I came to think of an afterlife, then what was the resurrection of Jesus Christ about? To many people, both inside and outside the Christian church, the resurrection of Jesus Christ means one thing: the promise of eternal life. In the catechism at the end of my *Book of Common Prayer*, the question "What is the significance of Jesus' resurrection?" has this answer: "By his resurrection, Jesus overcame death and opened for us the way of eternal life."

I asked a priest friend of mine about the significance of the crucifixion and resurrection, and he gave me the same answer: it's the promise of eternal life. When Christ appeared to the disciples after his death, it proved that death was not the end. My friend is a widower. He told me that to him, the resurrection meant that he would rejoin his wife after death, and that their love would continue for eternity. That promise meant a lot to him. I talked to another Episcopal friend about it, a gay man who had watched many of his friends die of AIDS. The promise that death didn't end our human existence and that he would see his friends again meant a lot to him, too.

In my return to God, I had learned the hard way to avoid assumptions about other people's faith. For one thing, people kept surprising me; if I listened carefully to them, my conjectures about what they thought usually turned out to be wrong. For another thing, I was insecure enough about my own faith, such as it was, to resent other people telling me what they thought I believed and why they thought I believed it. So I tried to hear what my friends said about joining their loved ones after death without assuming I knew exactly what they meant. The real question was, what did the crucifixion and resurrection of Christ mean to me, if anything? Could this story be about me?

The four gospels of the Christian New Testament told of a human man who acted as though he had the authority of God. Jesus didn't say, "This is just what I think, you might think differently," or "Here's one way of looking at things," or "Try this one on for size." He said it like he knew it was true. He cut across social boundaries; he ate with everyone, talked to everyone, touched everyone. He stood inside and outside Jewish law at the same time. When Jewish leaders tried to test him about the law, he answered, in effect, "You turn our law into a cage. The law is not a cage but a pair of wings. Use it and be free." He taught people, he healed people, he told odd stories. He broke the pattern. He confounded expectations.

Then he was arrested, tried, and executed. The gospel stories told of a man who lived an authentic life, true to what he believed to be right, and this life led him to an early, painful, and avoidable death. I imagined that Jesus of Nazareth had about as much free will as I did, and that if he had acted to preserve his life, he could have died an old man. Dying on a cross was an unexpected and inconvenient thing for the Messiah to have done. I could easily read much of the passion story as myth: the betrayal in the garden, the specific words Pilate and Jesus exchanged at the trial, the offering of vinegar and gall to the dying man. It wasn't hard for me to see these elements as attempts by the gospel authors to tell a spiritual rather than a factual story. However, I doubted if gospel writers added the crucifixion itself as an embellishment to Jesus' life.

He really died. And after he really died, in some way, according to the gospels and the epistles, he really came back. The story wasn't over. Most likely, none of the principal writers of the New Testament were contemporaries of Jesus of Nazareth; and yet, they all believed they had personal experience of Christ risen from the grave, and they all connected Christ to a real, live, human man who had died on a cross.

When I first returned to the church, it was a great puzzle to me that the central, defining image of the Christian religion was the cross. Not the image of the mother and child, though this was a powerful and familiar representation in Christianity. Not the descending dove. Not the burning flame. Not the bread and wine.

No, the defining image of Christianity was an instrument of torture and execution. The cross, where, as legend goes, Jesus of Nazareth died an agonizing death. Then, three days later, his corpse stood up and walked.

I thought the story was about overcoming death, and so I doubted it. I thought "eternal life" meant life after death, and that it was a bad central myth for a religion. Everything changed for me, though, when I started to focus on the "life" in eternal life, and when I defined "eternal" not as time without end, but as a state outside of time, not relevant to time. When that happened, the passion and resurrection of Jesus Christ became for me not a story about death, but a story about life. The eternal nature of this, real life.

For example, when I connected the passion and resurrection story to my compost pile, the cross as a symbol of Christianity became both right and terrible. The cross says that before I could live a new life, my old life would die. Before I could reach out and take the new prize, I had to be willing to drop whatever was in my hand now. Before I could become rich new earth to hold and feed new life, I had to be completely broken down and eaten by worms. It was going to be bad. At some point in the process, I might even cry out, "My God, my God, why have you forsaken me?" Then I

For Jews demand signs and Greeks desire wisdom, but we proclaim Christ crucified, a stumbling block to Jews and foolishness to Gentiles, but to those who are the called, both Jews and Greeks, Christ the power of God and the wisdom of God. For God's foolishness is wiser than human wisdom, and God's weakness is stronger than human strength.

—I Corinthians 1:22-25

would die, or some part of me would die. Then something new would stand up, something that couldn't be born without the life and struggles and death of what came before.

Jesus died and Christ rose. Christ is redemptive, getting me out of my cage so that I can be one with God. Christ shatters the porcelain cup. Christ is the crossroads. Christ says "choose."

I'm a former smoker, which gives me a ready-made story about death and resurrection in my own life. It's not far off to say that I was a smoker long before my first puff. I was still in high school, and I already had a mental image of myself smoking—the image of a sophisticated, tough young woman, about as different from how I appeared to myself in real life as she could be. My parents didn't smoke and neither did any of my friends, so for quite awhile I couldn't figure out how to get a cigarette and try that image on for size. However, I was always on the lookout. I carried matches with me, just in case. Then one afternoon it happened. On my walk home from school, out of sight of our house, there was a whole, unlighted cigarette lying on bare ground. I picked it up, lit it, and smoked it. The experience was a little disappointing; the cigarette didn't seem to do much for me. However, at about the same time the next day, I wanted something. The desire was physical, and I knew exactly what I wanted: another cigarette.

I was a smoker for the next fifteen years, until I finally quit after a series of ugly respiratory infections one winter. The physical addiction died hard. For more than a year after quitting, each and every day I felt that same, familiar longing through my veins and nerves, the longing for nicotine. Finally, the physical addiction died. It left behind a ghost of itself, a ghost that still occasionally brushed my neural pathways. The ghost was nowhere near strong enough to get me to start smoking again; it was more like the memory of desire than like desire itself.

If the physical addiction died hard, the image of myself as a smoker—that tough, sophisticated woman, someone who looked at life through narrowed eyes and a haze of blue smoke—died much harder. For years after quitting, I retained the inner image of myself opening a match book, striking the match, and lighting a cigarette. When this seductive woman, the smoker, was evoked, I wanted her to be alive; I wanted to smoke a cigarette. Gradually, she wasted away. I retained her ghost inside me, too, just as I retained the ghost of the physical addiction. However, eventually I stopped being seriously tempted to start smoking again.

Smoking was a habit I got into that was ultimately bad for me. It had to die; the pattern had to be broken. However, it served a purpose for its time. For one thing, that tough woman got to live in the real world for a while. Also, my will power received a good workout in the year and a half it took me to quit. The smoker died hard, then out of her tomb stepped the former smoker, a clear improvement. When I compared the story of Christ's death and resurrection to the story of nicotine and me, the parallels were obvious. Like the myth of the Virgin Birth, the Passion-Resurrection myth told the story of my life.

I have other examples from my life—better examples, to be honest—that parallel the story of Christ's passion and resurrection. The Christ story is a single, real-human, mythical enactment of every chance for rebirth I ever experienced, from the trivial to the grave. The problem is that I'm too ashamed to tell those other stories. I come off pretty well in the smoking story. A seventeen-year-old who lights up her first cigarette is an object of pity more than blame (unless she's your own kid, that is). When a friend kicks the habit, most of us offer congratulations, not contempt. It isn't hard to admit that I'm a former smoker. The other examples are different; I'm not willing to spill those guts. In Christian churches you often hear how Jesus willingly suffered and died an "agonizing and shameful" death on the cross for the sins of the world. At first I didn't see why his death was described as "shameful," but after censoring most of my own crucifixion stories from this book out of shame, I found the word surprisingly accurate. In real life, the seeds of redemption seem to take root in the rankest excrement.

In connecting the story of Christ to the passion story of my life, I came to respect the cross for its strength, its honesty, its willingness to face the terror and violence inherent in life. The cross both honors the sacrifice and celebrates the new life. The cross says, first, that something's going to die, and it won't be pretty.

Then comes redemption.

Acting out redemption

Religious myths tell about cosmic and human life in story form. In rituals, we get to act the stories out. Near the start of my second year at St. Paul's, I took part in a strange ritual. During a special Wednesday service not long before the vernal equinox, Mark, our priest, stood in front of the altar, a small bowl of ashes in his hands. The ashes were made by burning the greenery left over from the previous year's Palm Sunday service. One by one, each person in the congregation stepped up to him. When it came to my turn, Mark dipped his thumb in the ashes and drew a small cross on my forehead. While he drew the cross, he said, "Remember that you are dust, and to dust you shall return."

"Amen," I said, then like each other member of the congregation, I returned to my pew. The service continued.

That was Ash Wednesday, the first day of Lent. What followed was forty days of getting our perspective back, examining our hearts, trying to separate the wheat from the chaff. At the end of Lent came Palm Sunday, the day of Jesus' triumphant entry into Jerusalem. The congregation decorated the interior of the sanctuary and nave with greenery representing the palms laid down on the road to cushion his path. Here in the Pacific Northwest, we used ferns and cedar boughs to decorate our church on Palm Sunday.

Five days later, on Good Friday, the day of Christ's death, all the greenery was stripped from the church. Most was discarded, but a few fronds and boughs were set aside, labeled, and stored. Almost a year later, their dry, shriveled remains would be burned. Their ashes, ground with mortar and pestle and placed in a bowl, would be used to draw a small cross on each member's forehead at the Ash Wednesday service.

"Remember that you are dust, and to dust you shall return" wasn't something I wanted to be told every day of my life, but I didn't want to completely forget about it, either. A good, strong reminder once a year felt about right. Using the greenery from Palm Sunday reminded me that this was all connected together, our lives and deaths, our triumphs and disasters, our divinity and our ordinary humanness. The service for Ash Wednesday was designed to help me see again what's important. The intertwined elements of myth and ritual gave the service its power. When the priest drew that cross on my forehead and reminded me of what I am, then whatever it was I prayed to—the force of creation, the commonality of life, the hydrogen atom, gravity, or whatever—was palpably with me in the room.

At its best, religion does that kind of thing extremely well.

Chapter X

Return

I'm coming to the end of this book, but not, as far as I can tell, to the end of this great turn in my spiritual journey. My relationships to God and to organized religion don't feel static to me; they continue to evolve at a smart pace. It's hard to talk about where I am now in this process, since both "where" and "now" are rapidly moving targets.

Throughout the changes that have happened in my spiritual life in the last few years, some things about my life have stayed the same; others have changed. Some things appear the same on the surface and are different underneath.

For example, even though I'm now a bona-fide church lady, I still curse in everyday conversation. I started cursing when I left home for college, liked it, and never gave it up. Now that I have an active religious life, however, cursing feels different inside me. Now that the words mean something, I enjoy it a lot more. When I say, "For Christ's sake!" I mean something specific, and I enjoy saying what I mean so precisely, in all its layers. Out of courtesy, I do try to avoid cursing during church committee meetings.

Paying attention

A change that's happened both on the surface and underneath involves mindfulness: I'm trying to pay better attention to the other people in my life and to the non-human world around us. In some mysterious way, paying attention is close to the heart of the matter for me.

Paying attention to other people—real attention—doesn't come naturally to me. It's often hard to admit that I might not know another person as well as I think I do, to admit that the other person might have more in common with me than first appears. It's hard to see a human rather than a stereotype, to approach each situation with curiosity rather than a feeling that I already know all I need to know. I have to keep trying, over and over, again and again. I'm grateful that neither of my two churches ever lets me forget how humanness is shared among all people. In the sermons, social programs, and other church activities, both my churches often challenges my complacency toward other human beings. I think that's one of the things that a good church does well.

The other side of paying attention—paying attention to the non-human world around me—isn't emphasized so much in church, but it's also close to the heart of the matter to me. Since my renewed interest in spiritual life, I've tried to pay closer and closer attention to the way things are in the non-human world. For example, for the first forty years of my life I barely noticed the passing of the major seasonal days in the year—the solstices and equinoxes and the midpoints between them. Now those days are marked on my calendar, and I never let one pass without spending time outside in the woods or on a beach, trying to pay attention to the state of earthly home. To look closely, and then more closely.

At first glance, a saltwater beach, the panorama of sky, sea, and land, appears so vast and beautiful, it's like seeing all the beauty of the world at once. I have to look closer. Walk until my legs are loose, see how the land turns and rises from the sea. Stop walking. Look at the patterns of the waves coming in, the way they break on the stones. Look at the stones, their colors and fissures. Look at one stone, pick it up, feel its shape and weight. Look into the tide pools, the teeming border between water and land, the patterns and colors of life. Kneel down. Look closer to see it *all*, not only the translucent jellyfish, but also the flies crawling over the dog feces. Know that the rich, heady aroma comes not only from the wind off the salt waves, but also from the pieces of dead, stinking crab at my feet. In some mysterious way, whether on the beach, in the woods, turning the compost pile, or even here at my desk, this process of looking closer is near the heart of the matter for me.

I have a writer friend named Graham who has spent the last few years designing a new kind of boat. Graham wants a small, single-person boat that's light enough for him to haul to the beach in a trailer behind his bicycle. He wants to be able to launch the boat himself and then propel it through the water using a leg-and-foot powered mechanism of his own design. He wants his boat to be able to go fast—as fast as a kayak, if possible.

To test his design, Graham built a quarter-scale model and set up a towing tank for it behind his house. He designed a system of weights and pulleys to control the precise amount of power used to propel the model through the water for each test. He designed a reliable releasing mechanism so that he could mark the beginning of each test run, and he used a stop watch that measured the speed of the boat to the hundredth of a second. He did everything in his power to reduce the variables and produce the best data either to prove or disprove the theory behind his design.

But as he ran the tests, Graham found that he could not, in the end, control all the variables. The model was too big to be set up indoors; he had to run the tests outside. Sometimes the wind blew during a run. He found himself wondering, after some of those runs—Did that one count? Should I add that data to the pool?

At those moments, Graham became aware of yet another variable in his tests, and that factor was *hope*. He *wanted* his theories to be correct, and it was only when trying to decide which test runs to include that he became aware of just how powerful that desire could be. He had plans for his design, plans that went beyond his own, personal boat. If his design theories were correct, other people might want a boat like his. In his mind, he was already writing the book that told them how to build it. If his theories were wrong, that book might never be written.

So, he thought to himself, "That last run, when the wind kicked up and the water in the tank rippled against the prow of the model as it moved forward, and the results weren't quite what I hoped for—Should that run count? Or *not* count?" He became aware that he was looking for ways to invalidate trials that didn't give the results he wanted.

The experience made him understand for the first time what science was all about, and also understand why scientists sometimes fudge their data. The question "Does this run count? Should I write this number down?" was an ethical question, and the answer was neither obvious or easy. It was also a question he was going to face again and again, at every test run.

The answer Graham finally came to, after some painful soul-searching, may not have been easy, but it was very simple. The answer to the question, "Should I write this number down?" was always the same. "*Yes.*"

You've got to write the number down, he told me. You have to count *all* of the test runs, whether the wind is blowing or not. Only after you've gathered all the data, and noted all the conditions, can you step back and evaluate your theory with integrity.

"We generate all these ways of fooling ourselves," Graham said. "We generate this welter of fantasy, and we don't want to spoil our fantasies with cold, hard data." After this experience, he felt that science and its tools, when used as they are meant to be used, could be humanity's last, best shot at moving out of our clouds of self-deception and into the real world.

Science is getting knocked on all sides these days, not only from religious fundamentalists, but from all kinds of people who perceive science as arrogant, one-sided, and the source of the troubles that come with the technology it produces. It's true that individual scientists can be so arrogant and narrowly focused, they're blind to any but their own truths, and that new discoveries bring new problems with them. Still, I don't know many people who would refuse a biopsy for a newly discovered lump because they think science needs to be taken down a peg or two.

Religion gets knocked for the same kinds of reasons as science: for its arrogance, narrow-mindedness, and tendency to create more trouble than its worth. Religion is also accused of concealing reality under a comforting blanket of measureless faith—the flip side, perhaps, of the scientist for whom nothing can be real until she has measured it.

My own sojourn into religion has convinced me that good religion reveals rather than conceals. Religion is the soul in search of itself and its relationship to the cosmos. This journey requires looking at all of it: the joy and the sorrow, the beauty and the horror of life. We hope for the best; we want meaning and love to exist not only within ourselves, but in the very soul of the universe. At times this great hope might tempt us to pick and choose only the data that supports our desires. But in religion, as in boat-building, the design must be tested in all conditions. When I say that I'm trying to pay attention, and that paying attention means being willing to look at all of it, I think I'm trying for the same moment of clarity that Graham experienced when the wind blew all over his theory. Looking at all of it is what good science is all about. I believe that it's also what good religion is all about.

God of justice, God of truth

When, some years ago, I started to pray as an atheist, I needed to figure out who, or what, I was praying to. The task eventually led me back to organized religion, which I had abandoned for many years. After working on the problem awhile, I found that for me, the bottom line on God was creation itself. I was praying to whatever caused things to exist. I thought that it also inhabited those things. For me, God was both the prerequisite for existence and its animating, incarnating element.

God is that, without which, existence does not exist.

This definition satisfied me, and it still satisfies me. I think it describes what I pray to. In another surprising turn of events, my definition also helped me use more orthodox definitions of God in church without too much discomfort. Church definitions of God struck me as simply attempts to find a way to get a handle on God, to talk about God in a way that made sense to the people who wrote the definitions. Their terms might not be my terms. In some cases, their terms might be more a barrier than a help to me. But if I made the effort, I could usually find some meeting ground between us.

I still had problems connecting God to justice, truth, or love. Those characteristics seemed essentially human to me. When people assigned them to God, I thought they were creating God in a human image. I thought they were constructing a false God, so that people could see the world the way they wanted it to be, and not the way it actually is. This opinion of mine was a serious impediment to worshipping the Judeo-Christian God who showed up in my Episcopal church.

The way I figured it, if God was the basis of creation, then the nature of creation provided information about the nature of God. I had such a hard time with the idea of divine love and divine justice because the love I received from and felt for the people closest to me, and the justice I understood as an ideal in human relations, did not seem to be expressed in the universe as a whole.

My God was obviously not a God of justice on the surface of things, if by "justice" I meant in some way equitable, or fair. When we Christians pray before meals, we thank God for the food we are about to eat. If we think of it, we might pray that hungry people throughout the world also be fed. If there's a big disaster in the news, we might add, "And dear Lord, be with those in China who have lost their homes in the earthquake." Or "be with those in Central America suffering in the aftermath of the hurricane." In effect, we're praying for God to help those who are dying of dysentery and even starvation because their safe water supply and crops were destroyed in the hurricane. But a hurricane contains the very same forces that, in their more benign forms, provided us with the food now sitting on our table—the baked salmon, herb roasted new potatoes, asparagus vinaigrette, and cherry pie for which we are currently thanking God. The same forces that produced our food left other people dying of dehydration by the side of the road. If it's appropriate for me to thank God for my lovely meal, isn't it also appropriate for them to curse God with their last breath? The God who created this universe and a God of justice did not seem compatible.

And yet, a tremendous amount of Judeo-Christian language insists that the one God, the one Lord, is a God of justice. I doubted very much if the cosmos appeared any more "just" to the people who wrote the Psalms than it did to me, so their constant linking of God to justice puzzled and offended me. I disliked many of the Psalms for that reason.

> God is a righteous judge, and a God who has indignation every day.
>
> —Psalm 7:11

I could call my God "just" only at an extremely deep level. A certain kind of justice rules at a deep level of creation: the level at which all things are created, broken, changed, and recreated. In that respect, I am created equal to the gnat, to the lichen, to the asteroid, and to every other human being on earth. God is not fair in the same sense that we try to make our court systems fair; God is fair in bringing all things to existence. But I doubted if that was what the psalmist meant when he wrote, "The statutes of the Lord are just and rejoice the heart."

It's the same with love, only more so. The closest I could come, and this was with full awareness that I was anthropomorphizing God more than felt right to me, was to look at love at the same deep level that I looked at justice. At that level, I could say that God's creation was the expression of love—of atoms, and then molecules, and then cells, and then beings. I could say that God loves existence itself, equally happy with a human child and with the maggots and bacteria that would someday strip its human corpse. If God loves any of it, then God loves all of it. This is using the word "love" in full awareness that the term is loaded for us humans in ways that may have nothing to do with the forces of creation.

My interpretations of the connection between God and justice or love weren't particularly satisfying when it came to church. They were flatly contradicted in most of the Bible readings that I heard at St. Paul's on Sunday mornings. The Hebrew Bible states explicitly, again and again: God's justice protects the widow and orphan. God's justice smites the oppressor and raises up the oppressed. The psalmists and the prophets do not talk about how they are equal to lichen in the sight of the Lord. They talk about human justice, right here, right now.

I attended a small group discussion on the nature of God led by a retired dean of the Episcopal church. He quickly acknowledged that most of the human aspects of the Christian God were metaphoric. "God is not a *man*," he said, "and God is not a *woman*, and God is not a *chicken*. God is *God*." However, he also said that we must claim certain characteristics for our God, and justice was one of them. He used the word "claim." He said that, as religious people, we must be willing to claim justice as a characteristic of our God. It was a small group, and he was friendly enough, so I could have spoken up then, but I was silenced by his certainty and by the certainty of everything I heard around me in church. So I asked my questions to myself. "Why?" I asked myself. "Why *must* we?" I just didn't get it.

Now, a glimmer of a new way to think about that question is slowly dawning on me. The glimmer rises from a variety of sources. One source is the implications of a God who is the basis of all creation and inhabits all creation. Such a God, by definition, includes it all. Darkness as well as light. My God includes the sun that enables the potatoes to grow and the hurricane that destroys the farm. The God I pray to must contain both joy and sorrow, both pleasure and suffering, both justice and injustice.

Back when the Hebrew people emerged as a separate tribe in the area between Egypt and Assyria, the choices about God were much different than they are today. Today, we descendants of the Judeo-Christian traditions basically choose between God and no-God, between theism and atheism. Back then, every region had its own local gods. Certain big gods spanned regions. People also worshipped ancestral gods and gods that represented forces of nature.

The God of the Israelites said, "I am the one Lord, the Lord of justice. Have no other gods before me." When he said that, he offered a very real choice.

Some scholarship on the origins of Christianity presents Jesus' "Kingdom of God" not as the heaven that all good Christians go to after they die, but as a new way of life. A *chosen* way of life.

I was reminded of a quote from Ralph Waldo Emerson at the back of the Unitarian hymn book. Emerson said, "A person will worship something—have no doubt about that. We may think our tribute is paid in secret in the dark recesses of our hearts—but it will out. That which dominates our imaginations and our thoughts will determine our lives, and character. Therefore, it behooves us to be careful what we worship, for what we are worshipping we are becoming."

Here again was the idea of a choice. A conscious, ethical choice about how the God of all creation works in me.

I don't want to go back to lopping off the parts of God that I don't want to see or acknowledge. It's all God, and nothing I do or say can lop off any of it. Characteristics like love, justice, truth, peace—and hatred, injustice, lies, and animosity—are indeed human characteristics. That doesn't make them apart from God. Nothing is apart from God. It's just that they are not characteristics of a God "out there," but of the God "in here"—inside me. They are the parts of God that are human. As the human in question, I choose how these parts operate, how they are enacted in the world. I can't dump the responsibility for justice on God, as though God is somehow separate from me. Unfortunately—or fortunately—I have to be responsible for justice myself, because as a human being, justice or injustice is *my choice*.

How is God expressed through the great horned owl who lives in our woods? The owl hunts and kills its prey, feeds its young, and sleeps an owl's sleep. How is God expressed through the sun and rain that nurture the potato field? Through the hurricane that destroys it?

How is God expressed through me?

Because I'm human, I'm conscious . . . or trying to be conscious. That makes it a little different for me than for the hurricane. I choose. I choose how God comes out in me. If there is to be justice in the world, however weak, partial, inconsistent, and ineffective, I must supply it. When I do, God's justice moves from the depths to the surface. God acts in a moral fashion when I act in a moral fashion.

At first I feel cynical, afraid, and depressed when I think this way. The universe is vast. I'm a speck. The universe is eternal, or close to it. I'm gone in the flick of an eye. What impact can I possibly make? Regardless of what I do, the universe will still be an unjust place. Even within the confines of our little world, human justice is notoriously subjective and culture bound. One society's "justice" is another's abomination. Human justice doesn't seem to be one steady, unchanging Truth, but a roiling lake of ever-evolving truisms.

And yet, in my own world, the world immediately around me and the people I know, my actions make a difference. In some cases, a big difference. I can love. I can try to choose my own best vision of justice, and my love and efforts makes a difference. I can pay attention and tell the truth as I know it. That's all I can do. When I do, God has an opportunity to act for the good in a purposeful manner.

This is frightening stuff. I'm reluctant to look at it too closely. I'm afraid it presents a challenge beyond my ability and willingness to change. I'm a member of the greatest consumer society in history. Almost anything I do, from buying a pair of shoes to taking a Sunday scenic drive, raises questions of justice in our global economy. I want to buy whatever I want in blissful ignorance of the effects of my choices—it's the American way! And I want to leave my nation's economic policy up to my duly elected representatives, without having to think about it much myself. Economics is boring. But if my God is the God of justice, how can I close my eyes?

While I wrote this book, the process of figuring out what I wanted to say and then saying it became, in a way, my experience of God. To use Emerson's words, it dominated my imagination and my thoughts. It certainly demanded more than I expected when I started out, one of the characteristics often ascribed to God. Now that the book's almost finished, I feel as if I'm awakening to a new life. The funny thing is, in this new life, my first question is the same question I asked over a hundred pages ago. I've returned again to the beginning, but not unchanged. The entomology of the word *return* includes the idea of turning a piece of work in a lathe. In my return to a religious life, I realize that I'm not only the operator of the lathe, I'm also the workpiece. I've been rotated, cut, shaped, changed, and returned to my original position. This time, the question isn't about the nature of the universe so much as it's about the nature of me. I ask the question not so much from curiosity, as from fear, hope, and awe.

Who, or what, is my God?

Epilogue

The Episcopalians and the Unitarians

For the first two years of my two-church membership, I thought I had found the Holy Grail of organized religion. At St. Paul's, I got all the myth, ritual, beautiful liturgical language and church music that my heart desired. At the Quimper Fellowship, I explored spiritual life outside the bounds of traditional doctrine with the support of other free-thinkers like me. Coincidentally, I also got to witness the transformation of a church: during my first two years of membership, the Quimper Fellowship tripled in size, hired its first minister, and built its first church building using mostly volunteer labor from church members.

I got a kick out of people's surprise and puzzlement when I told them I was a member of two different churches. "Does that work?" they asked. "Don't your churches mind?"

I told them it worked great, and that my churches didn't seem to mind at all. In fact, they were proud of me. One Unitarian would introduce me to another, adding, "Margaret's also a member of the local Episcopal church." Or one Episcopalian would introduce me to another with the words, "And this is Margaret, our *Unitarian* Episcopalian."

Nobody in my two churches showed the smallest discomfort with my two-church membership, not even the clergy. Even when I was confirmed in the Episcopal church during my second year at St. Paul's—an opportunity for a little talk about commitment if ever there was one—no one so much as breathed the subject aloud. Before the confirmation service, Mark, my rector, introduced me to our bishop as a member of St. Paul's who also attended the local Unitarian church. The bishop thought that was a very interesting approach, and he hoped it worked out for me.

However, as my third year as a two-church lady began, the flaws in my approach were coming home. They emerged from a direction I didn't anticipate—from myself. I was proud of my unorthodox approach to church life, so it was hard to admit that membership in two different churches had its problems. But it did.

A church can be like a social club, containing your closest circle of friends. It can be like a service organization—you volunteer time to others and get help when you need it. It can be a place to find humility, wisdom, fellowship, contrition, inspiration, and even, occasionally, God. After two years in two churches, I knew one thing for sure: the greater my involvement in either church, the greater the return.

I took lay reader training in both churches. I joined the Worship Committee at St. Paul's. I led a class in spiritual poetry writing at Quimper. I gave talks on my spiritual journey at both my churches. I cooked my best dishes for the pot lucks.

I had become committed to the vision of each church, which meant I wanted to support that vision. One way to support a church is simply to *show up* on a regular basis. However, the deeper I went in one church, the harder it was to find time for the other. I missed half the services at each of my churches—more than half, because every once in awhile I stayed home on Sunday morning, if only to prove to myself that I still had the option. I divided my time and money between my two churches; as a result, I saw that I made only half the impact I might at each. I wanted to increase my involvement in both my churches but didn't have the time, energy, or money to do it. I saw how far I could go in either church if only I gave up the other ... but

I couldn't give up the other. I was torn in two by the dilemma of being both an Episcopalian and a Unitarian.

The solution appeared simple: quit one of my churches. But I'd gone so deep. The thought of leaving either was too painful to face. I was in the middle of a blackberry thicket, with ripe, sweet fruit all around me but no path out except through the thorns. I started to think that maybe more people didn't do this two-church arrangement because *it wasn't a very good idea.* That was humiliating to admit.

Finally, I got out of the thicket the only way I could see—by forcing myself through the thorns and getting hurt. I downgraded my status at the Quimper Fellowship from "member" to "friend," which meant that I still got the newsletter but was not an active member of the fellowship. I stopped attending Quimper more than one or two times a year. My issues with Christianity were too engaging; they were what I thought about, in or out of church. I was trying to discover my relationship to the myths and images of a religion I once thought I knew well, but now found as new and surprising as it was familiar. I had to be there, on the battlefield, to keep the discovery process going. For now, I would be an Episcopalian. If I walked away from the Christian church again, it would be because that process had taken me to a new place. At the moment, I felt that I was still getting to know the home ground of my ancestral religion.

Over time, my involvement at St. Paul's has waxed and waned. For almost a year, I wrote "op-ed" pieces about parish life for our newsletter. Having been trained as a lay reader, I volunteered to be a lector, which meant I read the Sunday lessons to the rest of the congregation about once a month. Mark Taylor, the rector who had welcomed me back to Christianity, retired near the end of my second year at St. Paul's, and our new rector (St. Paul's first woman priest) sometimes asked me to write parts of the liturgy for special services.

I still struggle to define my role in the parish so that it works for both my church and myself. I left the Worship Committee after a couple of years, convinced that whatever my role in the parish might be, it didn't include committee work. I volunteered for some things that I later regretted getting myself into, and I didn't participate in some things that I later regretted missing. As the months pass, my attendance on Sunday morning has become irregular and then occasional. However, my occasions aren't the traditional Easter and Christmas Eve services. I look forward to next Ash Wednesday, when I'll receive my annual reminder that I'm dust, and to dust I shall return. My other can't-miss service is on Good Friday—the sparsely attended Stations of the Cross, where I'll be reminded that God's Passion is also the human passion.

Even though I "chose" St. Paul's, the choice doesn't feel final. Whatever is happening between me and religion, it isn't over. However, just as I never expected to become a church lady after decades of happy atheism, I don't know what's coming now. The veil that covers the future of my religious life is drawn very close to the present moment. One thing about the future I think I can predict. I will never again leave the images, symbols, myths, metaphors, and stories of Christianity behind. In the process of rediscovering my religion, they have become my stories. They live inside me. They'll be with me, in some form, wherever I travel in the next stage of my journey.

This book began with a prayer and will end with a prayer. The prayer at the start of the book helped me cope with some political problems in my waking life. Recently, I wrote a prayer for a more homely reason: to help me fall asleep at night. One night, lying in bed with all the day's tensions and events whirling through my head, afraid it would be hours before sleep shut them out, I saw an image of such strength, it could almost be called a vision. The image was of Mary, the mother of Jesus. She stood tall above me, then leaned down and scooped me up as though I were a child crying on the floor. She held me to her breast, and I put my hand against her neck. All the cares of the day slipped away. In a few moments, I was asleep. The next day, remembering the image, it seemed to me that the woman who lifted me up was both Mary, the Catholic's Queen of Heaven, and Via, the female God I addressed in prayer before returning to the Christian church.

I brought the image back in the following prayer, which borrows from the Roman Catholic "Hail Mary" for its invocation:

> *Hail Via, full of grace—*
> *Pray lift me up in your arms,*
> *O Mother of God,*
> *and hold me to your breast.*
> *Amen.*

I like this prayer because it combines my ties to Christianity and my search for God outside the Christian fold. Sometimes I address it to Mary, and sometimes to Via. Either way, when I'm in bed with the cares of the day spinning through my mind, I pray this prayer, the Queen of Heaven lifts me to her breast, and in a little while, I fall asleep.

Other Interesting Books

Many books have influenced the way I thought about God, religion, and my own life of the spirit. Here are a few I particularly recommend.

Before I returned to organized religion, M. Scott Peck's writings were a great challenge and boon to my spiritual life. Everything he writes is worth reading. You might start with *The Road Less Traveled* (Simon and Schuster, 1978); *People of the Lie: The Hope for Healing Human Evil* (Simon and Schuster, 1983), and *The Different Drum: Community Making and Peace* (Simon and Schuster, 1987).

Mark Twain wrote brilliant, angry, funny satire on organized religion that rings as true today as it ever did. For the religious satire alone, check out *The Bible According to Mark Twain: Irreverent writings on Eden, Heaven, and The Flood*, by America's Master Satirist (Touchstone Books, 1995). For the whole wonderful experience, see *The Complete Short Stories of Mark Twain* (Bantam Classic, 1990).

Huston Smith's *The World's Religions: A Guide to our Wisdom Traditions* (HarperSanFrancisco, 1989) provides a generous, inclusive overview of all the major religions in the world today. I learned a lot from him.

When I first joined St. Paul's, *An Introduction to the Episcopal Church* by J.B. Bernardin (Morehouse Publishing, 1983) was just what I needed to get my bearings in a denomination that was new to me. The readings at the back of the Unitarian songbook, *Singing the Living Tradition* (Beacon Press, 1993) provide a wide sampling of

Unitarian and Universalist writings. In addition, the coursework for the "Building Your Own Theology" workshop described in Chapter Five is available through the Unitarian Universalist Bookstore at 25 Beacon St, Boston, MA 02108, (800) 215-9076.

The Christian Church has never been the monolithic block of dogma that it can appear to be from the outside. Marcus Borg's *The God We Never Knew: Beyond Dogmatic Religion* to a more Authentic Contemporary Faith (HarperSanFrancisco, 1998) contains some of the best non-doctrinal thinking from within the church today. For a more polemical approach to the current state of Christianity, see *Why Christianity Must Change or Die* by John Shelby Spong (HarperSanFrancisco, 1998). I can also recommend *The Comforting Whirlwind: God, Job, and the Scale of Creation* by Bill McKibben (William B. Eerdmans Publishing Company, 1994) for a new reading of the Job story that points out its relevance to our own place in the ecology of Earth.

We're fortunate to live in a time of groundbreaking Christian and Biblical scholarship. Many fine books in contemporary Christian scholarship have come out in the past few decades, and I'd like to particularly recommend John Dominic Crossan's *The Birth of Christianity* (HarperSanFrancisco, 1998) and *Jesus: A Revolutionary Biography* (HarperSanFrancisco, 1994). *Who Wrote the Bible?* by Richard Elliott Friedman (Harper & Row, 1987) is a readable, engaging work that summarizes current scholarly thought on how the first five books of the Hebrew Bible (Genesis, Exodus, Leviticus, Numbers, and Deuteronomy) were written and compiled. For a similar treatment on the first four books of the New Testament, see *Who Wrote the Gospels?* by Randel McCraw Helms (Millennium Press, 1997). And for a wonderful overview of the Bible, you won't find better reading than *The Good Book: Reading the Bible with Mind and Heart*, by Peter J. Gomes (Avon Books, 1996).

My favorite book on the mystical experience is *The Cloud of*

Unknowing (Image Books, 1973), a short guide on how to experience Oneness with God, by an anonymous medieval monk with a universal sense of humor. For a contemporary look at how we might break free from the patriarchal images of God that dominate Judeo-Christian orthodoxy, see *Reimagining God: The Case for Scriptural Diversity* by Johanna W.H. van Wijk-Bos (Westminster John Knox Press, 1995). George C. Williams's *The Pony Fish's Glow: And Other Clues to Plan and Purpose in Nature* (BasicBooks, 1997) presents a view of the nature of God from a scientific rather than theological point of view. I'm indebted to Williams for the insight about the poor design in human breathing and eating tubes that appears in Chapter Five.

Books on human psychology from a Jungian perspective helped me think in new ways about the human responsibility involved in a God of justice. Again, the field is wide and deep. I particularly recommend *The Not-Yet-Transformed God* by Janet O. Dallett (Nicolas-Hays, 1998), *The Creation of Consciousness* by Edward F. Edinger (Inner City Books, Toronto, 1984), and Carl Jung's classic *Answer to Job* (Princeton University Press, 1973).

About the author

Margaret D. McGee is a Port Townsend, Washington, writer who has many diverse talents and interests. As a "Master Writer" with Microsoft Corporation from 1987 to 1994, she was the lead and primary writer for many print and online projects, including *Microsoft Access Step-by-Step*, a best-selling book in the software market. Her one-woman monologue "Class of . . ." won Third Prize in the 2000 Port Townsend Playwright's Contest, and was produced as part of the 2001 Port Townsend Playwright's Festival in March 2001 and at the Creative Place Theatre in New York City (by Love Creek Productions) in October 2001. Her short prose and poetry have appeared in such publications as *Seattle Voice*, *Orion Magazine*, and *The Living Church*, and her villanella "September 23, Quimper Peninsula" won First Place in the 1999 Autumn Poem contest sponsored by *Byline Magazine*. Margaret has been award a fellowship residency at the Dorland Mountain Arts Colony for October 2002 (a nonprofit retreat center supported by the National Endowment for the Arts and the California Arts Council). Margaret has a B.A. in English from Miami University, Oxford, Ohio, and an M.A. in English from Ohio University. She served as Academic Advisor at the University of Puget Sound from 1979-1985, and as a Member of the Board of the Pacific Northwest Writers Association from 1985-1987.